modern RETRO

LIVING WITH MID-CENTURY MODERN STYLE

modern RETRO

neil bingham & andrew weaving

with photography by andrew wood

RYLAND
PETERS
& SMALL

London   New York

First published in the USA in 2000
by Ryland Peters & Small, Inc.
150 West 56th Street, Suite 6303
New York, NY 10019

10 9 8 7 6 5 4 3 2 1

A CIP catalog record for this book is available
from the Library of Congress.

ISBN: 1 84172 103 4

Senior designer   Paul Tilby
Senior editor   Annabel Morgan
Location manager   Kate Brunt
Picture researcher   Jenny Drane
Production director   Meryl Silbert
Art director   Gabriella Le Grazie
Publishing director   Alison Starling

Location research and styling   Andrew Weaving

Printed and bound in China by
Toppan Printing Co.

CONTENTS

introduction

The interest in creating period interiors for the home has a long and distinguished history. The ancient Romans acquired, interpreted, and copied furniture and objects, especially sculpture, from the ancient Greeks. Medieval emperors looked to the style of Imperial Rome. Many Victorians surrounded themselves with the trappings of a medieval existence. Beginning in the nineteenth century, the pace of historical revivals began to accelerate with such force that by today, in the early twenty-first century, the immediate past has become one of the ripest fields of interest. We have reached the era of admiring and collecting the Modern period, what we call **Modern Retro.**

In this case, Modernism may loosely be defined as the cutting-edge of the twentieth-century style in art, architecture, and design. At what point Modernism began, and when it ended—if it has ended—is a matter of controversy. For the sake of simplicity, we have taken the years between approximately 1920 and 1970 as our parameters. This is a logical span. It begins with the decade that witnessed the birth of styles like Art Deco—that middle ground between ornamented historic revivals and the unadorned—as well as such startling innovative movements as De Stijl and the Bauhaus. Our period ends with the 1970s—years of doubt and anti-Modernist trends, and the birth of Postmodernism.

OPPOSITE **Rare pieces in a Modern Retro setting, evidence of a collector's sharp eye. The table appears to be a unique hybrid piece from the office of Charles and Ray Eames in the 1950s: the top is from an Eames elliptical table and the dowel legs from the same designers' chairs of the period. A perfect match for the Dining Chair Wood (DCW), also by the Eameses.**
ABOVE **In a bedroom, a casual tabletop arrangement with early chairs by Alvar Aalto from the 1920s.**
LEFT **A Thonet chair of American production in a New York loft.**

THE RENEWED INTEREST IN THE MODERN RETRO LOOK HAS CREATED A MARKET FOR THE RE-ISSUE OF CERTAIN FAVORED OR REPRESENTATIVE PIECES.

The essence of Modern Retro is twentieth-century household items such as furniture, lighting and fabric furnishings, plus those innumerable useful and decorative items that stamp the individuality of the owner on an interior. Most of these owners are collectors, although many would deny this rather grand status and would prefer to say that they simply like to acquire good pieces from the Modern period. They are knowledgable about historical styles and developments within Modernism, recognize the classic pieces of each period, and know how and where to acquire them.

One advantage of collecting Modern Retro is that continued lines and re-editions of furniture, textiles, and other objects are available to create the style. Many classic twentieth-century pieces have never gone out of production. Most works, however, have a limited run, but the renewed interest in the Modern Retro look has created a market for the re-issue of certain favored or representative pieces. While some people might enjoy furnishing their homes with a new version of a bright white plastic lighting globe designed by George Nelson, others might prefer the yellowed and cracked original that retains an air of authenticity and history. It is a matter of choice.

OPPOSITE PAGE **Modern Retro tends toward minimalism. Here, reflected in a mirror, is a Jasper Morrison Glo-ball lamp of the 1990s—very reminiscent in its form of George Nelson's 1950s Bubble shades.**
LEFT **Modern Retro interiors can tell little white lies. This room is dominated by the La Chaise chair, which was designed by Charles and Ray Eames in 1948, although it did not go into production at the time. The fun fib is that this chair has only been put into manufacture recently, yet is already a Modern Retro classic.**

The owners of houses and apartments who create Modern Retro interiors do not strive to make a facsimile of the past, but rather to emulate and recreate its best or most enjoyable qualities. Their homes are not essays in nostalgia, but in the optimism that pervaded so much of the Modern period. You only have to look at any of the photographs in this book to see that Modern Retro interiors are, above all, about the present. Many of these rooms are in the vanguard of today's interiors, for Modern Retro is one of the hottest looks of the moment.

A single, cohesive thread ran through design between about 1920 and 1970. Within these fifty years, different styles came and went in rapid succession, yet viewed today, from our new century, this was a period of explosive energy and purposeful direction in art, architecture, and design. The term often used to describe this period is "Modern." Of course, the twentieth century witnessed counter-movements, too, particularly revivals of classical styles, but it is the Modern Movement that is the most highly appreciated today.

DESIGN DECADES

A 1950s-style Modern Retro interior. The 1951 Lady armchair, by Marco Zanuso, is a re-edition, but all the other pieces are vintage.

The main influence on today's Modern Retro look is the Modern Movement, which first emerged in the 1920s alongside another flowering of modern design ideas, Art Deco. Other styles were also popular in the interwar period, but today it tends to be only committed collectors with a specialized knowledge and a large budget who stray outside the realms of Art Deco and Modernism.

1920s & 1930s

LEFT **The interior of the small villa that Eileen Gray built for herself in the late 1920s on France's Côte d'Azur. The furniture is mainly by the architect and includes the Bibendum armchair, Transit chair, and Centimètre carpet.**
ABOVE **The furniture Eileen Gray designed in the 1920s and 1930s has only recently been appreciated by a wider public. Original pieces by Gray are rare, highly collectable, and very expensive. Re-editions, such as this Bibendum armchair, are beautifully made and true to the ideals of the vintage pieces.**
ABOVE RIGHT **First a student, then a master at the Bauhaus, Marcel Breuer is renowned as an architect and a designer. In 1925, aged only 23, he created the Wassily chair, an early exercise in tubular steel.**
BELOW RIGHT **During the 1960s and 1970s, re-editions and copies of Breuer's Cesca chair of 1926 were the favored dining chair of the moment.**

The term "Art Deco" derives from an exhibition held in Paris in 1925: the Exposition Internationale des Arts Décoratifs et Industriels Modernes. This event marked the emergence of the style that was to spread across Europe and take firm hold in the United States. Before World War I, Paris had been the fashion capital of the world, especially in *haute couture* and interior decoration. The Art Nouveau style was at its height. Art Deco, also sometimes called Art Moderne, developed from the nonhistorical approach of Art Nouveau, although its applied decoration was geometric rather than naturalistic in form.

Now Art Deco has become an all-encompassing term, used to cover the whole interwar period. True Art Deco objects and interiors, however, are sophisticated, graceful, and often exotic in flavor. High-quality Art Deco furniture is usually made from rich, densely grained woods, with furniture by the French designer Jacques-Emile Ruhlmann considered the finest expression of the style.

The Art Deco rooms of the period, especially those in the U.S., were often the work of interior decorators, a new professional breed. This interest in interior design was promoted through popular magazines, which brought the Art Deco style to a wider audience. The public, in turn, demanded mass-produced examples of the craftsman-made pieces that adorned the richer salons.

Mechanization was a prime inspiration in the creation of the advanced styles of the 1920s and 1930s. Although many Art Deco pieces attempted to give the appearance of being machine-made, they were usually painstakingly handcrafted and producing them was thus highly labor intensive. However, the Modern Movement, variously called Modernism and, in architecture, the International Style, confronted this dilemma head on by turning to the machine as its primary aesthetic. Technology was both its means and its nature.

Historically, the Modern Movement emerged from the nineteenth-century Arts and Crafts Movement, whose ideology was expounded by men such as John Ruskin and William Morris. In Germany during this period, the concept of the social responsibility of design—good, affordable design for all—was promoted through the Deutsche Werkbund and especially

ABOVE LEFT **A London interior from 1933, "modernized" by Ronald Dickens. The sash window reveals the room's age, but the square armchair, metal stool, and electric fireplace are thoroughly 1930s.**
ABOVE **An outstanding kitchen of the period: bright, sparkling, and efficient. The linoleum is laid in a geometric pattern; the cabinets are painted; and the appliances are very up-to-date.**

the Bauhaus school of design under the direction of Walter Gropius. New materials, methods, and techniques of factory production were used to produce unornamented, strictly functional, and almost industrial-looking objects for the home and office. Instead of the bulky, heavily upholstered furniture that was the norm for the period, lightweight bent tubular steel and sleek leather chairs were introduced.

LEFT **The famous all-white living room created in 1927 by the decorator Syrie Maugham for her own house in London's Chelsea. The room's surfaces and furnishings were all in various shades of white, brokenly reflected along the back wall by a tall folding screen made up of mirrored panels. The floor was covered by a specially commissioned Marion Dorn rug.**

BOTTOM LEFT **A French table lamp by Perzel, its metal shade reminiscent of a soldier's helmet.**

BOTTOM CENTER **The architect Mies van der Rohe designed this daybed, with its frame of teak and slender chrome legs, in 1930. It is available today as a re-issue by Knoll.**

BELOW RIGHT **A carpet by Da Silva Bruhns in deep Art Deco shades.**

THE CONCEPT OF THE SOCIAL RESPONSIBILITY OF DESIGN— GOOD, AFFORDABLE DESIGN FOR ALL—WAS PROMOTED BY THE DEUTSCHE WERKBUND AND ESPECIALLY THE BAUHAUS SCHOOL OF DESIGN.

ABOVE **This bathroom was installed in an old English manor house in the Kent countryside. The 1930s style is evident in the curved lines of the interior and fixtures.**

BELOW **A stool dating from 1930 by the master of bent laminated wood, Alvar Aalto.**

During the 1930s, the hard-edged look of the early Modern Movement mellowed into a softer aesthetic. Organic shapes were introduced into furniture, textiles, and tableware. The influence of Scandinavia had much to do with this gentler approach, as designers like Alvar Aalto experimented with bending and laminating the wood of his native Finland into supple, organic forms. Yet, Aalto's furniture still fell within the new laws of aesthetics, because his work was technologically advanced and "functional," a term favored by the Modernists for an object shorn of decoration.

The 1940s and the 1950s are contrasting decades in terms of arts, architecture, and design. The first decade was dominated by war, austerity, and discomfort; the following was one of relative peace, and saw a move toward exuberance, color, and the rediscovered pleasures of living. It is little wonder, therefore, that the Retro look of the 1950s is an extremely popular field of collecting today.

1940s & 1950s

World War II erupted in Europe in 1939 and quickly spread its destructive tentacles around the globe. Almost all industry and manufacture was diverted into producing goods that served the war effort. There was little time for the niceties of home comforts. Yet from these difficult times emerged a lively field of fresh ideas and practices. Wartime manufacture forced designers to adapt and create new materials that gave rise to improved methods of design production.

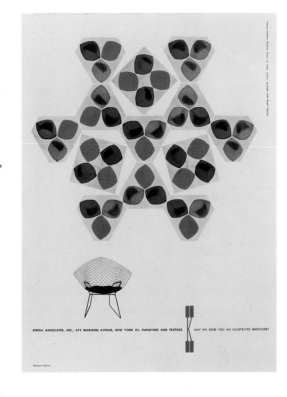

In the closing years of the 1940s, as the war-ravaged nations attempted to put themselves back together, technologically advanced countries that had had no fighting on their soil—such as the United States, Canada, and Australia—discovered that they had both the wealth and the expertise to cater for a sudden boom in population. Designers worked to meet the demand, which mainly came from the younger generation, for new consumer goods such as modern furniture, lighting, dinnerware, decorative objects, and household appliances. And while the very highest quality pieces and gadgets were expensive, the market soon adapted and began to produce cheaper imitations.

Although World War II had enforced nationalistic tendencies and loyalties, the rapid expansion in science and technology, another outcome of the war, began to shrink international barriers. Similarly, ideas on design and home decoration became internationalized. A glance through *Design for Modern Living*, one of the leading interiors books of the period, written by Gerd and Ursula Hatje and published in 1961, shows how akin contemporary apartments and houses of the period looked, whether they were in New York or Zurich.

If there is a look that sums up this period more than any other, it must be represented by the Case Study Houses. Begun in California in 1945, the idea of John Entenza, editor of the American magazine *Arts & Architecture*, the

DESIGNERS WORKED TO MEET THE DEMAND FOR NEW CONSUMER GOODS: FURNITURE, LIGHTING, DINNERWARE, DECORATIVE OBJECTS, AND HOUSEHOLD APPLIANCES.

A DESIRE TO HOLD ON TO THE PAST, COUPLED WITH SLOW ECONOMIC RECOVERY AFTER THE WAR, RESULTED IN MODERN DESIGN BEING TAKEN UP MORE SLOWLY IN EUROPE AND SCANDINAVIA.

Case Study Houses were a series of one-off modern dwellings designed and built over the next decade by forward-looking architects such as Richard Neutra, Pierre Koenig, Craig Elwood, and the leader of the pack, Charles Eames. These houses, lightweight in construction, with open plans and transparent walls, were decorated and furnished in complementary style. Furniture, fabrics, and everyday objects were either selected from high-quality international pieces or designed by the architects themselves. Many of these architect-designed works, most notably the furniture by Eames and George Nelson, are still manufactured and are today regarded as classics.

The 1950s was a decade that nurtured innovative design in specialized areas, with named designers leading their fields. In Italy, the architect Gio Ponti designed new forms in ceramics, glass, and furniture. Glass from Scandinavia had a timeless appeal, especially those pieces produced by

LEFT **When introduced in 1951, the Eameses' Wire Mesh chair had a variety of bases, as shown in this contemporary photograph. The chairs came fully upholstered or with a two-piece pad, which has since become known as a bikini.** ABOVE **A Wire Mesh chair is pictured here in a perfect early 1950s American kitchen, as featured in an ad from the Herman Miller furniture manufacturing company.**

studios such as Iittala and Nuutajärvi in Finland and Orrefors in Sweden. The Dutch firm Philips produced cosmic-looking lighting, while the abstract patterns of Midwinter tableware, many based on the newly discovered atomic structures of the day, kept homes abreast with the latest fashions.

By the late 1950s, it would appear that Modernism had triumphed. Yet it is easy to forget that the modern style had met fierce resistance from many quarters. During the 1950s,

BELOW TOP **The Homemaker pattern by Enid Seeney has become one of the most recognizable images of 1950s tableware. It is easily acquired today because enormous quantities were sold at Woolworth's. The pattern is of 12 Modern images, such as kidney-shaped tables and other modern furniture.**
BELOW CENTER **Considered more elegant was tableware of the period by Midwinter. This tableware often carried designs by well-known British designers like Jessie Tait, Hugh Casson and Terence Conran.**
BOTTOM **Sea Urchins, a 1945 fabric design by Ray Eames.**

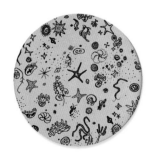

the opposition had been vocal, but increasingly these voices of resistance appeared anachronistic. In the U.S., where there was less of an historical tradition than in the Old World, Modernism made quick inroads. There was something natural about its taking root in a country that had always reveled in novelty and quick acceptance of new ideas as the natural outcome of what was perceived as the God-given right of freedom of choice.

But in those countries with a rich cultural heritage it was impossible to throw away centuries of traditional fine craftsmanship. How was it imaginable to ignore the beauties of a past that constituted the very foundation of a nation's psychological security? Grandmother's Regency sideboard, Uncle George's Staffordshire figures—men and women had given their lives in a war to preserve such objects and the history they represented. This desire to hold onto the past, coupled with slow economic recovery after the war, resulted in modern design being taken up more slowly in Europe and Scandinavia. It also meant that during the 1950s interior design in such countries as Britain, Italy, the Low Countries, Scandinavia, France, and Germany was eclectic. An Egg chair by Arne Jacobsen could fit comfortably alongside an eighteenth-century clock, while a Victorian chair might be upholstered in an abstract furnishing fabric by Lucienne Day.

Yet in recent years, when the design expressions of the 1950s have been re-appreciated and re-evaluated, an attempt has been to make this decade appear homogeneous, sleek, and all-encompassingly modern. The labels applied to the style of the 1950s reflect this: The New Look, Contemporary, Mid-Century Modern, Fifties Style, The Atomic Look, to give but a few. This decade's unadulterated and optimistic view of Modernism is what Modern Retro today is most often about.

ABOVE, RIGHT, AND BELOW RIGHT **Three chairs from the 1950s with fin-style armrests made from the continuous curve of the frame rather than the traditional method of attaching separate arms. The uplifted arms of this chair (ABOVE) reminded its designer, Arne Jacobsen, of the wings of that queen of all birds; hence its name—the Swan. From the same year, 1957, and also by Jacobsen, is the similar but much grander Egg chair (RIGHT). Although Modern in inspiration, its enveloping shape and wing-tip back continues a long tradition of chair design. The most famous of British patio chairs was the Antelope (BELOW RIGHT). Used prominently at the 1951 Festival of Britain in London, Ernest Race's chair, with its ball feet looking like molecular forms, reflected the new interest in atomic structure, one of the exhibition's principal design themes.**

Why is the 1960s such a confusing decade to pin down? Perhaps because it was a period of provocation, revolution, and extremes. The decade began quietly enough: postwar austerity was vanquished, the Western world seemed to be moving together in harmony, and Modernism was firmly established. But the seeds of disintegration and fragmentation were already sown, bursting forth as the decade unfolded: cries of "Ban the Bomb" were turned into "Make love, not war" by anti-Vietnam War protesters, the Beatles went from clean-cut to psychedelic, and water beds kept springing leaks.

BELOW Early 1960s furniture, such as the Sling sofa by George Nelson dating from 1963, shown here both in profile and from the front, featured the early Modern elements of tubular steel framing and sling leather upholstery. As the decade progressed, Modern furniture production took a turn when plastics became more dominantly used.

1960s

BELOW In post-war Britain, Harrods, the *grande dame* of department stores, promoted Modern furniture. There is a strong element of the decorator's touch in this 1962 room display.

In design, the first years of the 1960s calmly carried on from the preceding decade. The confident, clean lines of the postwar era continued to dominate goods and interiors. Many leading designers and manufacturers of the 1950s sustained and developed their individual styles. Moreover, design hits from the 1950s often did not enjoy popularity until the next decade because, as is often the case, it takes time for a new aesthetic to percolate into a wide market.

In the U.S., right through the 1950s and 1960s and beyond, furniture companies like Herman Miller and Knoll International produced chairs, sofas, office furniture, and storage units by designers such as Charles and Ray Eames, George Nelson, and Harry Bertoia. Not until the end of the 1960s were these names challenged by the anti-Establishment movement.

One of the most significant features of the mid-1960s was the shift away from America as the focus of hot new design. The world awoke suddenly to find that "Swinging London" was

RIGHT By the late 1960s, the circle, along with rounded edges on sharp profiles, had become a fashionable and favorite look. In this living room of the period, the wide circular base of a glass-topped table sits on an animal hide and forms the central focus for a seating area that consists of a pair of sofas with scooped-out shapes. The bottom half of the modular adjustable wall units have openings with quadrant corners. All-white rooms were also a popular aesthetic of the late 1960s and early 1970s.

For the finest contemporary furniture—both elegant and comfortable—come to the Furniture Galleries at Harrods. The setting shown here is one of many. Furniture also will you have as wide a choice.

Harrods

the new capital of style. The English were fueling a consumer society whose teenagers abandoned themselves in discotheques to the sounds of the Fab Four, Herman and the Hermits, and the Rolling Stones. The baby boomers had grown up and become "the younger generation," running in and out of the groovy boutiques up and down the King's Road, Carnaby Street, and Portobello Road. Skirt lengths were a major national topic of discussion as they rose to the mini, dropped to the midi, and then plunged to the maxi.

This was a period of radical social change. And it showed, especially in the world of design. In Britain, the visual stimuli that created the images of Pop became an overriding concern. As a consequence, two-dimensional aspects came to the fore: bold and vibrant posters, graphics, wallpapers, textiles, and paint colors—coverings that swathed great areas in bewildering patterns and

ABOVE **Hanging basket chairs were part of the new interest in all things Eastern and Oriental. The hippie movement, epitomized by the Beatles going to India to learn yogic contemplation, was especially eager to use furnishings that challenged conventional taste. This is a stylish adaptation of an alternative look.**
RIGHT **Used in the byline of this 1968 advertisement for Sanderson, the major textile manufacturer, "sensation" and "happen" were buzzwords of the drug culture of the 1960s.**

crazy perspectives. Such exuberance first appeared in London boutiques like Mary Quant's Bazaar, then Biba, then in such wonderfully named venues as Granny Takes a Trip. The wider market found its link to the new design aesthetic through Habitat, the furniture and home furnishings store opened in 1964 by the greatest design entrepreneur of the post-war years, Terence Conran. Habitat shops spread throughout Britain, selling their own lines or bringing in well-designed and affordable household goods from France, Italy, and Scandinavia.

Two artistic movements dominated the 1960s—Op and Pop—and these are the principal looks upon which many Modern Retro collectors of this period concentrate. Op grew out of the Op Art movement, which was championed by the British painter Bridget Riley, whose bold canvases, mainly in black and white, are of such intricate geometric patterns that they make the head spin. The link between Op, the psychedelic drug

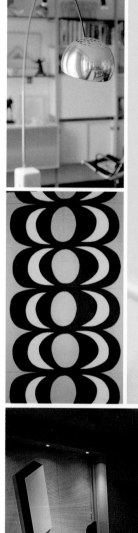

ALTHOUGH BRITAIN WAS THE CENTER OF MANY OF THESE NEW STYLE MOVEMENTS, MUCH OF THE BEST FURNISHINGS AND HOUSEHOLD PRODUCTS CAME FROM ELSEWHERE. FURNITURE AND GLASS OF EXCEPTIONAL QUALITY AND DESIGN CONTINUED TO POUR OUT OF SCANDINAVIA AND ITALY.

culture, and interior design was immediately apparent. Drop your tab of LSD, close your eyes, and the world becomes Op. When you open your eyes, the living room is part of your trip. Swirling distorted grids of circles and diamonds pattern walls and ceilings—it's the wallpaper and curtains; lay back on something with a fluffy, soft texture yet a decidedly queasy pattern—it's the carpet and cushions; and let your head weave in and out of planets, stars, and asteroids—it's the globe chairs, spherical television, and geodesic lights.

Pop was another decidedly anti-Establishment movement, a rejection of the Modernism that the design establishment had revered so much that it now seemed dated and old-fashioned. Peaceful opposition arose, yet in a decidedly aggressive manner. Hippy culture, the popular youth movement, believed that it was creating a backlash by picking up on those elements that Modernism had reviled. And chief among the enemies of the old guard was historicism.

What could be more outrageous than going back to the very design movements that the early Modern Movement had done battle with? Art Nouveau and Art Deco became new favorites—styles saturated with ornamentation, patterns, and colors that broke all the rules of Modernism.

Although Britain was the center of many of these new style movements, much of the best furnishings and household products came from elsewhere. Furniture and glass of exceptional quality and design continued to pour out

ABOVE LEFT In the 1960s, Italian lighting began to take on Pop-fantastic shapes. This giant pill capsule, Pillola by Casati & Ponzio, is an allusion to the widespread drug scene.
BELOW LEFT Textured glass by Geoffrey Baxter for Whitefriars, for the popular end of the market.
ABOVE RIGHT The enormous Arco floor lamp by the Castiglioni brothers, dating from 1962, is like a shooting star.
ABOVE CENTER Kaivo, designed by Maija Isola for the Finnish textile house Marimekko. Such Op Art textiles were used not only for fabric furnishings, but were also stretched and framed like works of art.
OPPOSITE ABOVE The inflatable Blow chair, an Italian design of 1967, came with a puncture kit for repairing the vinyl.
OPPOSITE With more than 14 million sold since first introduced in 1963, Robin Day's Polyprop chair, here in the children's version, can be seen in every corner of the world.
BELOW RIGHT Bold graphics decorated walls in the 1960s and early 1970s. This photograph appeared in the dining room section of Conran's The House Book (1974).

ABOVE LEFT **Red means revolution.** In this dining room, the shutters are painted in target graphics and the chairs are by Vico Magistretti, popularly sold in shops like Habitat. Pinpoint lighting was a new feature for interiors of the period.

ABOVE RIGHT **A clash of colors** in a 1960s living space. Communal and laidback living was the ultimate in groovy.

ABOVE FAR RIGHT **Kitsch or Kulture?** The lava lamp, first introduced in 1963, is today undergoing a revival and is available in a variety of space-rocket shapes.

LEFT **Psychedelic living:** neon light sculptures are implanted beneath a glass floor and reflected in a mirrored wall.

RIGHT **A dramatic Op Art effect** joins this living area, with its pair of bright green fiberglass Pastil chairs, to a sunken conversation pit.

of Scandinavia and Italy. And, on the back of its strong chemical industry, Italy now entered the new world of plastic goods. Designers like Joe Colombo plugged into the wild and wonderful shapes of the era, fashioning not simply home interiors, but entire home environments—integrated room settings for the laidback generation.

Because Op and Pop are such overwhelming and uncompromising styles to live with, dazzling in their brilliance and ornamentation, Modern Retro enthusiasts of today are usually selective in their choice of pieces rather than attempting to recreate the authentic look in a contemporary interior.

DESIGNERS LIKE JOE COLOMBO PLUGGED INTO THE WILD AND WONDERFUL SHAPES OF THE ERA, FASHIONING NOT SIMPLY HOME INTERIORS, BUT ENTIRE HOME ENVIRONMENTS.

ABOVE **Verner Panton's plastic stacking Panton chair, first introduced in 1960, sits in a Modern Retro interior of today. In 1960s design, sensual body forms, celebrated in everything from furniture forms to Mick Jagger's tongue logo, celebrated the period's sexual revolution.**

In the 1970s Modernism died. Or so the story goes. In 1977, Charles Jencks published his groundbreaking book, *The Language of Post-Modern Architecture*, in which, with tongue firmly in cheek, he gave with precision the time, date and place of the death of the Modern Movement: 3:32pm, 15 July 1972, in St. Louis, Missouri. At that moment, a large housing estate built in the 1950s was demolished by controlled dynamiting. Modernism had failed and was about to be replaced by the Post-Modern.

1970s

Historicism, which had always been lying beneath the surface of the Modern Movement, came back into its own during the 1970s. The revivals of the 1960s had fueled this change in attitude. At the beginning of the 1970s, the reinterpretation of such styles as Art Nouveau and Art Deco continued apace. And collecting nineteenth-century furniture and objects—Victoriana, as it was called then—was undertaken in a spirit of fun and daring. But collecting it was, and soon the pursuit became a serious one, with large public exhibitions and academic books devoted to designers who had come to be considered the "pioneers of modern design": William Morris, Charles Rennie Mackintosh, C.F.A.Voysey, and Louis Tiffany. Ordinary people were learning design history and creating a new style of interior in homage.

Post-Modernism was Modernism layered with historical and cultural references. These references could sometimes be quite blatant, such as Capitello, an Italian chair in the shape of an Ionic capital designed by Studio 65 in 1972. Although sometimes the allusion was subtle, as Post-Modernism developed into the 1980s, guided by the Italian group Memphis, objects tended to cite past styles directly—Michael Graves's Biedermeier-inspired furniture being one example.

The 1970s witnessed a return to earlier, more stable ideals, but with a twist. In many ways, this was a result of the economics of the decade. The first of several energy crises hit in 1973 as Middle Eastern powers began to flex their international muscles by holding back and price-jacking their oil reserves. Even the mighty U.S.A. felt the pinch as unemployment, recession, and labor unrest took hold. How different the world suddenly seemed. In contrast to the

ABOVE RIGHT **Designer chic in a London penthouse. The neutral colors are given a High-tech edge with the polished metal column and finishes. There is also a quality of fragile transparency, with a clear acrylic-backed Plia chair at a glass-topped table and a collection of crystal obelisks.**
ABOVE FAR RIGHT **A living room with the oversized richness of sectional furniture in leather and a wall of mirror glass typifies the expensive consumer look of the 1970s.**
BELOW RIGHT **A chic setting with six leather-covered chairs, including a pair of high-back Aluminum Group lounge chairs by Eames. Elements of the Pop Art movement survived into the 1970s, such as the use of a dragonfly kite as decoration in this room.**
BELOW FAR RIGHT **With plenty of space to breathe, two Bastiano lounge chairs, with boxy wood frames and deep leather upholstery, designed by Tobia Scarpa in 1969.**

ABOVE RIGHT **In the same vein as the disposable blow-up and paper furniture of the 1960s is Frank Gehry's Wiggle side chair of 1972, made of laminated cardboard.**
RIGHT **A reaction set in during the 1970s against the wild and rebellious look of the previous decade. This took two basic forms: one was radically anti-design and the other, exemplified by this living area setting with its conservative furniture, purgative and safe.**

heady days of the 1960s and early 1970s, when the force of protest had turned opinions on civil rights and the Vietnam War, helplessness and apathy had now set in. The optimism that followed the Second World War had been reflected in interiors filled with bold new colors, patterns, and shapes.

The 1970s was a more doubtful and insecure decade, and Post-Modernism developed partly in response to these feelings of distrust and disillusionment. Here was a style that called for a back-to-basics approach to design. Classic elements gave reassurance of the continuance of stability and good taste.

For a brief period before Post-Modernism took off in the late 1970s, its immediate predecessor was an Italian movement known as Anti-Design. As its name implies, and the products

attest, the designers believed that good design was no longer possible. They produced lumpy chairs and angular sofas with sharp edges that are virtually impossible to sit down in. Yet, for all this supposed madness, Anti-Design had qualities that were highly decorative and humorous. Today, these radical design statements are collected more as works of sculpture than pieces of furniture; objects simply to be admired because they are so hopelessly unusable.

ABOVE **The flat roof loved by many Modernists began to disappear in the 1970s, to be replaced by sharply raked roofs that gave interiors greater architectural definition. This interior is evidently an architect-designed space, with its evident love of materials such as the boarded wooden ceiling and ceramic tiled floor. Natural and cool earth tones were extremely popular in the 1970s.**

The other mainstream interior design force that emerged during the 1970s was High-tech, which stood in direct opposition to Anti-Design. High-tech returned to the basic tenets of early Modernism, adopting a mass-produced, utilitarian, almost industrial look. Venetian blinds were metallic, floors were rubber-studded, spotlights were clipped on polished metal shelves, and colors were primary. This was very much an architectural movement, lead by prominent British architects such as Michael and Patty Hopkins, Richard Rogers, and Norman Foster.

But the majority of room settings of the late 1970s sought a fresh and comfortable look, utilizing only subtle touches of the Postmodern and High-tech. Furniture and other objects were given more space to breathe, and sleek white interiors were considered the epitome of style. Antiques began to be reintroduced into interiors, but this time without the ironic overtones with which they had been associated in the previous decades. And Modern design classics of the twentieth century were given pride of place; pieces like Charles Rennie Mackintosh's tall-back dining chair or Gerrit Rietveld's red/blue chair, the most famous work of the De Stijl period.

In Britain during the 1960s and much of the 1970s, the bible for home furnishings at the more affordable end of the market was the popular Habitat catalog. However, in the late 1970s, a new gospel came to challenge the

RIGHT **By the 1970s, Modernism had become mainstream. Its cutting-edge and revolutionary character had been accepted and tamed. Good taste began to decree which pieces of furniture of the Modern Movement were to become design classics, as in this interior set with pieces of 1930s furniture such as the Le Corbusier-Charlotte Perriand chaise longue and a pair of Marcel Breuer's tubular steel Wassily chairs. In many respects, Modern Retro has its roots in this decade.**
BELOW **A quartet of stools and chairs by Anna Castelli Ferrieri, dating from 1979.**

BELOW FAR LEFT **In the 1960s and early 1970s, Verner Panton became obsessed with the circle and its permutations—translated in three dimensions into globes—creating textiles, furniture, and this Panthella lamp based on its form.**
BELOW LEFT **In the late 1970s, white interiors represented a cleansing of the frenetic color schemes of previous years.**

THE OTHER MAINSTREAM INTERIOR DESIGN FORCE IN THE 1970S WAS HIGH-TECH, WHICH STOOD IN DIRECT OPPOSITION TO ANTI-DESIGN. HIGH-TECH RETURNED TO THE BASICS OF EARLY MODERNISM, ADOPTING A UTILITARIAN, ALMOST INDUSTRIAL LOOK.

old: the IKEA catalog, which eventually had a very wide distribution after the Swedish company opened stores in Germany and then across Europe and North America. Drawing upon the classic tradition of Scandinavian Modernism, IKEA helped to create an extremely affordable yet design-conscious home lifestyle that continues to influence the way the majority of people choose and buy their household possessions right up to the present day.

INGREDIENTS
of the Modern Retro look

Modern Retro is a high-style game, and some familiarity with the trends, styles, and objects of the Modern period is necessary in order to create the look. Some people may think that only rare original pieces are used, and at first glance this may appear to be the case. Most followers of the look acquire Modern classics, but these are just as likely to be new re-editions as originals. And they also seek out, or come across in their travels, unique and desirable items—perhaps a vintage chair by an unknown designer or a vase in the style of a master potter but unsigned.

New, vintage and re-edition pieces are the ingredients of the Modern Retro look. Here, a new sofa by Antonio Citterio for B&B Italia is combined with a vintage LCW chair and re-edition surfboard table, both by Charles and Ray Eames.

THIS PAGE **Authentic French
1950s furniture. The Antony
chairs, exceptional in this case
for having slipcovers, and the
occasional table are by Jean
Prouvé. The staggered
Bibliothèque behind is by
Prouvé and Charlotte Perriand.**
OPPOSITE PAGE ABOVE **A dining-
room set by Robsjohn-Gibbings.**
OPPOSITE PAGE BELOW LEFT
**Jacobsen's Series 7 chairs have
never gone out of production
since their introduction in the
mid-1950s.**
OPPOSITE PAGE BELOW RIGHT
**Although nowadays chiefly
remembered for her early
Modern chairs in tubular steel,
Charlotte Perriand was also
responsible for many designs
with a craftsbased inspiration,
like these chairs.**

Modern Retro interiors take as their focus classic furniture of the twentieth century. Pieces of good contemporary furniture designed between the 1920s and today can sit harmoniously together in a room, if chosen and arranged confidently. And just a few carefully selected items will set the style and the look for the whole interior.

furniture

There are some pieces of Modern Retro furniture that were recognized as classics from day one, while others are only now enjoying an elevation to classic status as they are rediscovered and Modern Retro collectors begin to use them in their interiors. In recent years, some pieces have become so familiar that they almost border on cliché, like the Eames lounge chair 670 and its matching ottoman, first produced in 1956.

It is a wonderful irony that one of the greatest furniture classics of the twentieth century is a humble café seat designed in mid-nineteenth-century Austria: the Thonet bentwood chair. In the 1920s and 1930s, and again in the 1960s, when Victorian furniture became all the rage in the Pop period, this elegant and sturdy yet lightweight little chair cast its spell over the design establishment. Even today it is still possible to find one for a reasonable price, although so many variations of this chair have been produced over the last century and a half that some versions are now of museum rarity and, accordingly, museum value.

The Thonet bentwood chair served as a great inspiration for the early Modernists, and the architect and designer Marcel Breuer even worked for the Thonet company in the 1920s, bending tubular metal to create several chairs that have remained stars of the Modern canon. One was his

RIGHT **A 1960s retro dining room with a set of Cesca chairs and a Saarinen pedestal table.**
FAR RIGHT **Cushions with coverings by Salvador Dali on a vintage American two-seater.**
BELOW LEFT **The leather-upholstered luxury of Le Corbusier and Perriand's Grand Confort chairs.**
BELOW RIGHT **The sensuous steel frame of Mies van der Rohe's Barcelona chair.**
OPPOSITE PAGE LEFT **The Eameses' La Chaise of 1948 was put into production by Vitra only in 1990.**
OPPOSITE PAGE RIGHT **A low Jean Prouvé daybed.**

simple Cesca chair, fashioned from a single length of metal tubing that twists to form the arms, seat support, and precariously cantilevered base. This chair, a staple item in Habitat catalogs of the 1960s and 1970s in Britain, represents an instance where Modern desire finally achieved Modern attainability. Ideologically, this piece of furniture was designed for mass production—Breuer always intended the chair to bring good design to a wide audience. However, in the 1920s, when the chair was designed, technology was not advanced enough to allow the design to be quick-assembled, with the result that the chairs had to be virtually handcrafted, and they were therefore expensive. It was not until the 1960s that the Cesca chair began to be mass-produced and became an affordable design for a wide market.

Many other classics of the interwar years, extremely labor-intensive to manufacture and made from costly high-quality materials, have remained exclusive and expensive pieces. One such example is the chair designed by Mies van der Rohe

MANY OTHER CLASSICS OF THE INTERWAR YEARS, EXTREMELY LABOR-INTENSIVE TO MANUFACTURE AND MADE FROM COSTLY HIGH-QUALITY MATERIALS, HAVE REMAINED EXCLUSIVE AND EXPENSIVE PIECES.

for the German Pavilion at the Barcelona Exhibition of 1929. With its luxurious padded leather upholstery and polished steel frame, the Barcelona chair was later to become synonymous with the reception areas of chic 1950s office buildings and affluent penthouses. Today, due to the popularity of the Modern Retro look, they are again appearing in the same type of locations.

In the 1950s, enterprising furniture firms began to forge productive and long-lived relationships with leading designers. In the U.S., two companies stand out above all others: Herman Miller and Knoll International. The greatest furniture designers of the period, Charles and Ray Eames, designed for Herman Miller, and in the U.S. the company still owns the rights to their pieces today. Eames, working in collaboration with his wife Ray, pushed forward technological frontiers by constant experimentation with molded plywood and plastics. Dining- and living-room chairs, stacking chairs, screens, desks, wall units: any piece by the Eameses is highly collectable today.

IN THE 1950s, ENTERPRISING FURNITURE FIRMS BEGAN TO FORGE PRODUCTIVE AND LONG-LIVED RELATIONSHIPS WITH LEADING DESIGNERS OF THE PERIOD.

his slanted Platform bench from the previous year has been making a comeback in recent years and finding its way into many of today's design outlets.

Knoll International also had its coterie of stars, chief among them Eero Saarinen and Harry Bertoia. Saarinen was the architect responsible for the most celebrated airport building in the U.S., the TWA terminal at New York's JFK, and his best-known pieces have a distinct sensation of flight about them—for example, his Tulip chair and Pedestal table of 1957, which rise and float upon a tapering base. Bertoia's greatest contribution to the period was his Diamond chair, with its wire grid structure, which was so successful that the designer was able to turn fulltime to his favored activity of sculpting.

From 1946 to the mid-sixties, the director of design at the Herman Miller Company was George Nelson, an enormously influential architect and designer who was responsible for some of the best-known pieces of the post-war years. His Ball wall clock of 1947 had a distinctive face of little globes on wires in place of the numbers—styling borrowed from fashionable atomic imagery—and was widely copied, while

ABOVE **An international design mix, with the yellow Coconut chair by American George Nelson, the orange Swan two-seater by Dane Arne Jacobsen, and a coffee table by Frenchman Paul Frankl. The glass is mainly Italian.**
ABOVE RIGHT **The warm hues of wood soothe sleep. A sculpture by Dennis Cummings rises upon a Robin Day Hilleplan chest of drawers.**

THIS PAGE Cool easterly breezes blow through the open balcony door of this 1930s beach house. A giant House of Cards by Charles and Ray Eames can be arranged and rearranged like kinetic sculpture. The DAF chair comes from George Nelson's Swagged-Leg Group. The owner of this weekend home keeps in touch on his one-piece Ericofon.

OPPOSITE AND LEFT **This short-haired pussycat has found a cozy bed on a long-haired sheepskin casually thrown over Hans Wegner's Flag Halyard chair. Wegner's easy chair, dating back to the early 1950s, has a frame of painted and polished tubular steel wound with flag halyard, a natural rope used for hoisting and lowering boat sails.**
RIGHT **The cast-iron column and radiator of this New York loft loom over a pair of low-backed chairs by Charlotte Perriand.**
FAR RIGHT **A detail of Perriand's Chauffeuse Japonaise chair shows the hooked frame firmly clamping the chunky but tailored back cushion.**

GENERALLY SPEAKING, PIECES OF GOOD MODERN FURNITURE DATING FROM THE 1920s TO THE 1950s WILL SIT HARMONIOUSLY TOGETHER IN A ROOM.

Scandinavian furniture design of the 1950s, which was some of the very best of the decade, was dominated by names such as Hans Wegner, Finn Juhl, and Arne Jacobsen, all of whom were Danish. Much of their furniture was made from teak. This lovely wood, imported from the Philippines, took on new meaning in the hands of Danish craftsmen. Danish Modern, as this movement was dubbed, was characterized by its organic lines and natural materials, and was a look that found great favor in the U.S. However, the classic chair from Denmark was of molded plywood à la Eames: Arne Jacobsen's Series 7 chair, also known as the 3107, which are still made by the same enterprising Danish furniture manufacturer, Fritz Hansen.

Generally speaking, good Modern furniture dating from the 1920s to the 1950s will sit harmoniously together in a room as long it is arranged with conviction. There is a continuous line of development within this design timespan, with the achievements of the postwar years building on the lessons of the interwar period. But during the 1960s, especially as the decade progressed, the shapes and materials of many of the

THIS PAGE **The solid shapes and forms of a collection of wooden and ceramic vessels contrast with the airy openness of the metal mesh of Bertoia chairs.**

leading pieces began to take on a very different look, and putting pre-1960 and post-1960 furniture together in a room setting can sometimes have its problems.

The Polypropylene chair, by the British designer Robin Day, is a piece that manages to bridge the gap. First produced in 1963, this inexpensive work of excellent design has sold more than any other chair in history. It has an enduring quality, falling halfway between the idealistic world of the Eameses and the throwaway decade of blow-up plastic furniture, paper dresses, and cactus-shaped coat racks.

During the 1960s and 1970s, Italy became the home of radical design. Designers came together in cooperatives, issued manifestos, and bombarded the public with exaggerated and fantastical works. One such group, Archizoom, dismissed the functional aspects of Modernism, instead choosing to revisit and pervert elements of Art Deco, the Modern Movement, and kitsch 1950s style. One of their most outrageous pieces was the Safari "livingscape" from 1968: a hard, polyester-framed seating arrangement covered in imitation leopard skin.

However, such wild fantasies were at the extreme end of the furniture spectrum. The everyday house or apartment of the 1960s and 1970s tended toward the conventional. For those who collect this period today, Sixties and Seventies furniture offers an opportunity to revel in the exotic and

FAR LEFT **The squared-off frame of this French chair holds in place the curved woven seating of patterned textured rope.**
LEFT **Objects take on new and interesting forms when placed on highly reflective surfaces such as the black laminated top of this Noguchi table. The smaller circular base mirrors the larger tabletop.**

THIS PAGE **An arrangement of wooden furniture stands upon a poured white latex floor. The daybed is vintage Aalto, its mattress covering slightly distressed. To harmonize, the owner commissioned floor lamps in 1930s style.**
RIGHT **The organic shape of the large Robsjohn-Gibbings table was popular in the 1950s. Its layered plains with undulating edges are like a topographical relief or lapping waves. Behind, Arne Jacobsen's Swan chair is a similar essay in organic unity, with back, sides, and arms all of a single piece.**

ABOVE A basket chair by Nanna
Ditzel hangs above a High-tech
rubber-studded floor. Poul
Kjaerholm's PK22 chairs, with
their leather seats and backs,
have been in production since
the mid-1950s.

LEFT Three types of furniture—
nesting tables, recliner, and
stool—all designed by Marcel
Breuer and manufactured in
Britain during the 1930s by the
Isokon Furniture Company.

THIS PAGE **The pair of armchairs were originally in one of the famous Modernist houses on the Weissenhof estate in Stuttgart, and were shipped to England when the owners emigrated. The U-shaped Penguin Donkey bookshelf, designed by Egon Riss in the 1930s to hold Penguin paperback books, is a re-issue.**

ABOVE RIGHT **A Brancusi-inspired stool sits alongside a molded plywood Aalto stool with a high back.**
CENTER RIGHT **A host of onlookers in a Bruce McLean painting gaze passively at a collection of Retro pieces.**
BELOW RIGHT **A molded plastic Eames side chair is pulled up to a built-in breakfast bar.**

THIS PAGE **The Eames fiberglass-shell rocking armchair was sold by Herman Miller between 1950 and 1968, then for the next 14 years only offered as a gift to employees of the company who became parents. The paper lamp on spindly legs is a Noguchi re-edition.**

OPPOSITE PAGE ABOVE **In this apartment in New York, Knoll-styled 1950s office furniture has been re-used in a household setting. The color mix, with a painting like a giant textile, is an effective backdrop.**

OPPOSITE PAGE CENTER LEFT **This collector's love of postwar British design is evident from the Robin Day chest of drawers and Festival winged armchair, first designed for the opening of the Royal Festival Hall, London, in 1951.**

OPPOSITE PAGE CENTER RIGHT **With woven wicker seats perched on thin metal legs, these barstools have a 1950s sensibility.**

OPPOSITE PAGE FAR RIGHT **There is nothing more space age than transparent furniture, such as this chair from Laverne International's Invisible Group, in production between 1957 and the early 1970s.**

OPPOSITE PAGE BELOW RIGHT **Earth tones predominate in an apartment in London's Barbican that holds a 1970s rosewood cocktail cabinet and an Eames Soft Pad Group swivel chair.**

BY A QUIRK OF TASTE, IT IS THE FANTASTIC PIECES OF FURNITURE FROM THE LATE 1960s AND 1970s THAT TODAY EXCITE THE HIGHEST PRICES IN AUCTION ROOMS AND IN THE GALLERIES OF MODERN DEALERS.

bizarre. Why choose a traditional sofa when today it is possible to acquire the extra-terrestrial Djinn sofa designed by Olivier Mourgue and used in the space station scene of Stanley Kubrick's 1968 film epic, *2001: A Space Odyssey*? By a quirk of taste, it is these fantastic pieces of furniture from the late 1960s and 1970s that today excite the highest prices in auction rooms and in the galleries of modern dealers. Archizoom's Safari seating unit, for example, may well sell for a price as much as five times that of Robin Day's Form Group modular seating of two decades earlier.

LEFT **Deep, dark, and rich; this corner has as its focus the family heirloom of an armoire. The Eames Time-Life stool looks like a giant chess piece on the glossy floorboards. The stool, designed in 1960, can serve as either a seat or a low table. This example is one of four designs available. Originally made of solid walnut, the stool is still in production but is composed of several pieces of wood, laminated and pinned together.**

BELOW **Raised and sunken living spaces were popular concepts in the 1960s and early 1970s, offering a choice of positions for sitting and reclining. The Contour sofa by De Sede is here set against a custom-made wall unit: integrated in the pierced panels are an air conditioner and, at the lower right, a music center.**

RIGHT **The long, low Forum sofa by Robin Day, with wonderfully distressed leather cushions, stretches beneath a row of louvered windows in a 1970s London house. The AX chair is Danish, designed by Peter Hvidt and Orla Mølgarrd-Nielsen in 1950. Its two-tone coloring is a result of combining light teak with darker beech.**

lighting

Lighting is one of the most creative aspects of putting together the Modern Retro look. Designers of the Modern period have created a wide spectrum of lighting, suitable for anything from task work to romantic effects, from the classic 1930s Anglepoise desk light to the Castiglionis' soaring Arco.

In the 1920s, electricity became a cheap commodity for the first time. This encouraged its use in the household setting and opened up a huge market for new electric goods. Electricity transformed the way people lived. It allowed greater scope when it came to planning the internal arrangements of buildings, because electric lights could be positioned anywhere in a room, illuminating even the darkest corners. Electricity made it possible to open up interiors instead of having to cluster seating areas around the sources of light or heat.

The new and unprecented brightness of electric light made objects look flat and shadows less prominent. Much Art Deco and early Modern Movement furniture compensated for this drawback by accentuating the luminous qualities of materials. Art Deco furniture, with its shiny lacquers of black and Chinese red, took on jewellike qualities under electric lighting. Similarly, the chrome and glass favored by the Modernists sparkled and gleamed under electrical illumination. However, the difference between Art Deco and Modern Movement light fixtures could not be greater. Art Deco lighting was mainly in the form of uplighters—floor

RIGHT **Three types of lamp in a Modern Retro living room: an early 1950s table model by Philips, pierced wall sconces and an elegant floor lamp by John and Sylvia Reid.**
OPPOSITE PAGE ABOVE **Like a watchful god, an African mask from the 1940s looks down upon this Deco Retro corner. The American lamp, with its splayed wooden base, sits alongside a French Deco sofa with brass-tipped feet. The table is made of macassar wood and the sofa of rosewood.**

lamps and torchères—which were extremely popular in the 1920s and 1930s, and were available in various shapes ranging from classical pillars to the famous elongated bronze snake designed by Edgar-William Brandt, which stood straight up on its tail with its hissing head grasping the shade. In contrast, the Modernists preferred their lamps resolutely minimal and unadorned, their ideal being a tubular pole on a base with a V-shaped glass shade. The Modernists' interest in new technology and materials gave rise to innovative designs such as the Anglepoise desk lamp, with its spring-loaded balancing action, invented by English engineer

George Carwardine in 1932 and subsequently produced by the Norwegian company Luxo. The Anglepoise is still in production today.

After World War II, the United States, Sweden, and Italy came to dominate the field of lighting design. Prominent designers who often worked in other areas such as architecture and furniture turned their talents to lighting. As a result, lamps and shades emerged in new, inventive shapes, and methods of lighting the home became more creative.

The designer George Nelson and his fellow American Isamu Noguchi can be credited with one of the most influential looks in lampshades. In 1952, the Howard Miller Company began to produce Nelson's Bubble shade, a taut plastic skin stretched over a wire frame that came in a variety of organic shapes. In the same year, Noguchi, drawing upon his Japanese heritage and working with Knoll International, produced the first in a series of Akari lampshades, delicate forms constructed from handmade paper. Inspired by the bulbous ribbed shapes of both designers, companies such as the British firm Rotaflex were quick to produce a line of similar shades designed by John and Sylvia Reid. By the late 1960s, when the influence of the Far East was making a considerable impact on Western design culture, the traditional Japanese paper lampshade was readily accepted as an inexpensive alternative to the designer originals, and it has been popular ever since.

ABOVE LEFT **A space-age sputnik ceiling pendant hangs in the entrance hall of a Victorian house.**
LEFT **An Italian glass mushroom lamp sits atop one of a pair of 1956 Quadraflex speakers designed by Charles Eames.**

LEFT **Two adjustable floor lamps whiten a cool white room furnished with highly collectable period pieces from the 1950s. The lamp with the tubular mesh shades was designed by John and Sylvia Reid for the British company Rotaflex Lighting. Both of the chairs are by Robin Day. In the corner stands an elegant storage unit by Frank Guille with plastic laminated sections.** RIGHT **A collection of flea-market finds are carefully arranged and illuminated by an industrial lamp.**

The Nelson and Noguchi shades are both very popular in the Modern Retro home, and modern re-issues are now in production. However, many lamps from the same decade, such as the PH series by the Dane Poul Henningsen, have never gone out of production. Working for the lighting firm Louis Poulsen, Henningsen was responsible for the famous PH5 pendant lamp of 1958. An update of his PH table lamp of 1933, this hanging light was created from layered painted aluminum cups that hid the bulb while reflecting its illumination and thus avoiding dazzle and glare. Henningsen went on to create a spectacular chandelier version, a nucleus of clustering metal leaves, aptly named the Artichoke.

The Italians brought all the forces of modern sculpture to lighting design. In the postwar years, Gino Sarfatti designed almost all the products for his lighting company Arteluce. There is something practical and straightforward about Sarfatti's lamps, qualities that are perhaps to be expected from a designer who trained as an aeronautics engineer. His 600 table lamp, for example, dating from 1966, is like a garage mechanic's torch on a beanbag base, it is both stable and allows for extreme lighting angles.

LEFT **A cluster of enameled metal disks on the shade of this French floor lamp is contemporary with Op Art effects of the 1960s. The large Lady armchair by Marco Zanuso is a re-edition, as is the smaller molded plastic Sitzgeiststuhl chair that was first constructed in wood by Heinz Rasch in 1927.**

BELOW LEFT **A shade with petals influenced by the flower-power of the hippie movement.**

THIS PAGE **Simplicity meets theatricality in a contest between two types of lighting. The standing task lamp is Italian, a bare bulb on a metal rod. The corner chandelier is a glittering confection by Verner Panton from his Fun Lamp series of the mid-1960s.**

OPPOSITE PAGE ABOVE LEFT **A bedroom is given Japanese minimalism with a paper lamp by Noguchi.**

OPPOSITE PAGE ABOVE RIGHT **Dappled light falls through a curtain of plastic disks at a bathroom window.**

OPPOSITE PAGE BELOW LEFT **A detail of Panton's lamp of shell disks that shimmer and tinkle like wind chimes.**

OPPOSITE PAGE BELOW RIGHT **Psychedelic lighting effects are created by shining rays of light at a mirror ball.**

Sarfatti sold Arteluce to the rival Italian lighting manufacturer Flos in the early 1970s. Flos had some of the biggest names in architecture and design in their stable, including the lighting superstars Achille and Pier Giacomo Castiglioni. These brothers were responsible for a wealth of lighting classics, including the Luminator uplighter of 1954, with a lightbulb perched at the end of a long metal tube on a tripod, and the 1962 Arco, a chrome bowl-shaped shade held at the tip of an enormous arching metal rod anchored in a marble block.

In the late 1960s and 1970s, serious elements of design often meshed with the witty and irreverent side of Pop Art and Anti-Design. The Italians continued to lead the field in lighting during this period. Funky lights emerged, such as the Ultrafragola mirror by Ettore Sottsass, which, with its neon tubes within a border of undulating plastic, can illuminate a small room.

In the 1970s, a new form of lighting, the tungsten-halogen bulb, was introduced. Originally used for retail and exhibition lighting, the light of the tiny, white halogen bulb is so dazzling

FLOS HAD SOME OF THE BIGGEST NAMES IN ARCHITECTURE AND DESIGN IN THEIR STABLE, INCLUDING DESIGN SUPERSTARS ACHILLE AND PIER GIACOMO CASTIGLIONI, WHO WERE RESPONSIBLE FOR MANY LIGHTING CLASSICS.

that it is used almost exclusively for background and directional lighting. Designers have had a field day exploring its possibilities for home use. Undoubtedly the most famous fixture to use the halogen bulb was also one of the earliest—the Tizio desk and table lamp of 1970, designed by Richard Sapper and manufactured by the Italian company Artemide. With its perfectly balanced weights and counterweights, this lamp became an instant classic.

TOP LEFT **A pair of mid-1950s Venini glass light fixtures designed by Massimo Vignelli.**
ABOVE LEFT **This shade was handmade to match the vintage base of thick Italian glass.**
ABOVE **Glowing lamps by Piero Gilardi from 1967 resemble molten boulders.**
LEFT **Every piece, including the floor lamp, is by Danish designer Nanna Ditzel. Her work is in the gentle tradition of Scandinavian Modernism.**
ABOVE RIGHT **Poul Henningsen's classic PH5 pendant.**
RIGHT **Panton's elegant Panthella lamp.**
FAR RIGHT **A sinuous 1950s lamp snakes up the wall.**

A floor covering ties a grouping of furniture together. The owners of this London house specially commissioned this rug to fit in with their Art Deco furniture. The pattern is very 1930s, with its thin line moving in an abstract formation, in the style of such well-known textile designers as Marion Dorn and Evelyn Wild.

For many people, textiles are an overwhelming passion. A chair may be an object of sculptural beauty, but a textile holds more tactile appeal. And, with their woven or printed patterns, textiles demand to be considered thoughtfully, as if contemplating a painting for its use of color or ingenuity of composition.

rugs and textiles

Strangely enough, textiles and rugs are sometimes seen as the poor relations of larger or bulkier household items like furniture or lighting. Perhaps this is because they are flat and two-dimensional, and thus easier to overlook or ignore. Yet a number of famous Modernist designers created innovative textiles and rugs, and at the 1925 Exposition Internationale des Arts Décoratifs in Paris, many textiles were on show. The most popular motifs were abstract or stylized, the majority showing overlapping squares and circles. At first, these bold new textiles were manufactured by exclusive firms, but new mass-production methods meant that geometrics became a style that spread quickly, infiltrating a market previously dominated by a taste for the floral.

The Bauhaus design school actively encouraged textile design and manufacture, a consequence of the determination of early members of the institution to update Arts and Crafts ideals. Walter Gropius, director of

the Bauhaus from 1919 to 1928, furnished his office with a large rug and wall hanging in bold geometric patterns. Several students from the Bauhaus such as Anni Albers and Lena Bergner went on to become influential textile designers.

The newfound vogue for abstract patterns in printed textiles that arose from Art Deco and the Bauhaus meant that traditional woven textiles became extremely fashionable from the 1930s well into the 1960s. These fabrics, usually made on large industrial looms, emphasized textures and patterns that were repetitious and thus subtly abstract. A variety of materials were used, such as silk, nylon, linen, and wool. Scandinavian countries and countries like Ireland that had a long tradition of weaving produced particularly beautiful examples.

The economic slump of the 1930s increased the cost of materials, but the introduction into the market of a cheap new synthetic, rayon, created a whole new look in upholstery fabrics. Rayon had a silky sheen that shimmered under electric light, and it could be dyed easily. Dyes also improved during this period, becoming

THE NEWFOUND VOGUE FOR ABSTRACT PATTERNS THAT AROSE FROM ART DECO AND THE BAUHAUS MEANT THAT WOVEN TEXTILES BECAME VERY FASHIONABLE FROM THE 1930s ON.

ABOVE LEFT **This textile design, with baskets, birds, and bowls that look like wire sculptures, was designed by Marian Mahler and manufactured by David Whitehead Fabrics in 1953.**
ABOVE **This cotton print by Mahler was inspired by the most popular textile design of the 1950s, Calyx by Lucienne Day.**
RIGHT **Haddon, designed by Maj Nillson for David Whitehead Fabrics.**
FAR RIGHT **The wavy lines of a radar screen served as the model for this 1950s pattern.**

OPPOSITE PAGE LEFT **In a New York apartment designed by the architectural group The Moderns is a series of new textiles by Judy Ross inspired by mid-century style. Light from a window is diffused through an aluminum folding screen hung with delicately embroidered leaf motifs.** OPPOSITE ABOVE RIGHT **A 1950s chest of drawers by George Nelson stands at the edge of a hand tufted rug by Ross.** OPPOSITE BELOW RIGHT AND LEFT **In a decidedly American tradition, Ross's design for this bedspread is aligned with the layered patterns created by Frank Lloyd Wright.** BELOW **Pillows and bedcovers with bold abstract patterns.**

more resistant to fading and wear. After World War II, new synthetic yarns for upholstery fabrics began to appear, including acrylics, polyesters, acetate, and, most influential in 1950s interiors, vinyl. Furniture manufacturers like Knoll International were instrumental in presenting these new materials in a favorable light.

During the 1950s, colors, although brighter than previously, were usually limited to a restricted number in each textile run. After World War II, in many devastated countries, this was due to economic necessity.

But in the U.S. a limited palette was considered fashionably avant-garde. Cloth often had a pattern that left some of the background unprinted, like paper showing through under a drawing. Well-known textile designers such as Ray Eames made a beautiful virtue of this look.

Printed cottons made a revival as an everyday upholstery fabric in the 1960s, and patterns began to go wild. Influenced by Pop artists like Andy Warhol, fabrics appeared with large surface patterns, flowers being a popular theme. Fashion designers such as Christian Dior and Mary Quant entered the textiles market, designing their own bed and bath linen. One of the most successful international manufacturers was the Finnish firm Marimekko, whose leading designers like Vuokko Nurmesniemi and Maija Isola helped shape Pop fashions.

Original textiles from the Modern Retro period can be difficult to track down. There are some survivors, of course, but often the heavy daily use of rugs, cushions, or upholstery fabrics meant that such items became worn or faded and were subsequently replaced. One solution is to purchase new fabrics that are in keeping with a Modern Retro interior. Sometimes large textile companies like Schumacher and Sanderson have continued

NOW THAT MODERN TEXTILES AND RUGS ARE SO POPULAR AND COLLECTABLE , MANY OWNERS PROUDLY HANG THEIR ACQUISITIONS ON THE WALL AS IF THEY WERE TAPESTRIES OR PAINTINGS.

ABOVE LEFT **The Viennese designer Jacqueline Groag worked for many years with the Wiener Werkstatte before moving to England and producing fine textile designs such as this one, dating from 1952.**
BELOW LEFT **A pair of cool blue and beige cushions made for Heal's by Barbara Brown in the 1960s.**
RIGHT **A Groag pillow sits on a sofa covered with Mourne Check, a hand-loomed cotton and flax tweed by the great Norwegian textile designer living in Northern Ireland, Gerd Hay-Edie.**

ABOVE **A circular rug, in Pop Art fashion, attributed to Verner Panton. The Egg chair complete with its matching ottoman are Arne Jacobsen classics dating from 1958.**

to manufacture a limited line of earlier designs. And now that Modern Retro is an established look, today's designers are creating textiles that take their inspiration from the Modern Movement. Some dedicated devotees of the Modern Retro look even have textiles woven or printed to historical patterns using original materials—an expensive but satisfying enterprise.

Now that modern textiles and rugs, especially those designed by such well-known names as Eileen Gray, Ray Eames, and Lucienne Day, are so collectable, many owners hang their acquisitions on the wall as if they were tapestries or paintings. This allows the items to be appreciated as the valuable objects they are, and eliminates unnecessary wear and tear.

Considering that utility and functionalism were two of the greatest virtues espoused by the early Modernists, it is ironic that many of the most important glass pieces of the twentieth century are purely decorative and absolutely unusable. Take

LEFT A companion pair of Venini glass bottle and vase match in color and 1950s period style the steel fronts of a George Nelson cabinet. ABOVE Deep cut, clean edged with heavy bases, Italian glass vases and bowls make bold collections. Like many glass pieces of the twentieth century, they are—form before function—simply admired objects.

RIGHT **Ribbon-trailed bowls and vases, designed by Barnaby Powell and made by London-based James Powell & Sons of Whitefriars between 1932–1940.**

Ingeborg Lundin's Apple vases, designed for the Swedish company Orrefors in 1957. A bubble-shaped vase with only the smallest of openings for a mouth, this beautiful piece might perhaps hold a single flower, but cleaning the interior is all but impossible. This vase is simply an exquisite work to be admired—glass as a work of art.

Such pieces of art glass grew out of two very different strands of glassmaking that coexisted during the 1920s and 1930s. One was decorative, the other plain. The master of decorative glass during this period was the French designer René Lalique. By the 1920s, Lalique had risen to fame with his delicate designs in the Art Nouveau style. Investing in modern production methods, such as a stamping press to create high-relief molding, enabled Lalique to swiftly adapt to the heavier and chunkier forms of Art Deco while still retaining a definite sculptural realism.

Objects made of glass are among the most highly desirable pieces found in the Modern Retro interior. Shapes, colors, and forms vary from the delicate and sensuous to the bold and sharp-edged. Today, rare studio pieces may command high prices, but a great quantity of mass-produced Modern Retro glassware is still easy to find and much of it is enormously collectable.

glass

Far simpler in appearance were the glass products designed for a more utilitarian market, such as the coffeemakers and tea sets by the Bauhaus-trained Wilhelm Wagenfeld. The elegant simplicity and practical aspects of such pieces soon began to influence developments in the field of art glass. One example is Alvar Aalto's Savoy vase of 1936. Reliant upon pure form rather than the theatrics of exquisite blowing or cutting, the Savoy vase has an undulating shape said to be reminiscent of the frozen lakes of the designer's native Finland. This vase is now almost a fetish in the Modern Retro home, as can be seen by its reappearance in every design shop in recent years.

Other Scandinavian glassmakers were influenced by the determined simplicity, organic shapes, and abstract vocabulary of Aalto's work, and Scandinavian glass companies, many of which had been around for centuries, suddenly found a new lease on life. Celebrated Scandinavian glass designers such as Kaj Franck and Timo Sarpaneva worked for a variety of companies—Nuutajärvi, Orrefors, Kosta Boda—bringing their individual style to each. Another Scandinavian glass superstar was Tapio Wirkkala, who began working with the Finnish workshop Iittala in 1946, creating thin, free-flowing vases that look like melting lumps of ice. Although Wirkkala stayed with Iittala until he died in 1985, he also enjoyed great success designing for Rosenthal in Germany and Venini in

ABOVE **Hourglass shapes were common in 1950s design, from light fixtures to the nipped-in waists of ladies' suits made fashionable by Christian Dior.** BELOW **A cheap and cheerful tumbler from the 1950s. Also used on wallpapers and textiles, leaves and other natural forms were a popular pattern of the period. The decoration on these machine-made glasses is of screen-printed enamel.**

OTHER SCANDINAVIAN GLASSMAKERS WERE INFLUENCED BY THE DELIBERATE SIMPLICITY, ORGANIC SHAPES, AND ABSTRACT VOCABULARY OF AALTO'S WORK, AND SCANDINAVIAN GLASS COMPANIES, MANY OF WHICH HAD BEEN AROUND FOR CENTURIES, SUDDENLY FOUND A NEW LEASE ON LIFE.

OPPOSITE PAGE **Glass on glass. An arrangement of continental and Scandinavian glass sits on a glass table top from the early 1950s. The table frame is made of rod metal softened with a coating of rubber.**
ABOVE **The two smallest of these glass bottles are by the Danish glass manufacturer Holmegaard. They were created by Per Lütken, the company's chief designer in the 1950s.**
LEFT **The fragility of glass makes even the less expensive pieces attractive.**

Italy. Today, it is still easy and extremely affordable to grace a Modern Retro sideboard with an original and very spirited Wirkkala glass design from 1966 – simply by purchasing a bottle of Finlandia vodka.

Until about the mid-1960s, vases, bowls, drinking glasses, and carafes from Finland, Denmark, and Sweden were all the rage in fashionable design-conscious circles. Scandinavian glass design moved from strength to strength during these years. The glass produced had something almost classical about it—the forms were simple, abstract, and wonderfully understated; and the pieces were always beautifully crafted.

LEFT **Tall decanters with outsized bulbous stoppers were made by the Venetian glass manufacturer Venini as well as the Finnish glassmaker Kaj Franck for Nuutajärvi.**
RIGHT **This glass bowl with balls attached to its outer surface is a fun oddity.**
OPPOSITE **A collection of Scandinavian glass dishes on a glass top table by Noguchi.**

ITALIAN GLASS DESIGN, WITH ITS EXAGGERATED GOOD LOOKS AND BRIGHT COLORS, WAS VERY DIFFERENT FROM THE WORK BEING PRODUCED BY GLASSMAKERS IN SCANDINAVIA.

During the 1950s, glass companies in countries like the United States and Britain tended to imitate the fashionable Scandinavian look. The London firm of Whitefriars Glass, for example, produced enormous quantities of heavy colored glass in the Scandinavian Modern style during this period, and although they are extremely collectable, such pieces are still reasonable in price, making it easy to acquire and compose large arrangements of them; accordingly, they are very popular in the Modern Retro interior.

Concurrent with the rise of Scandinavian glass came a new dawn in Italian glass design, which, with its exaggerated good looks and bright colors, was very different from the work being produced by glassmakers in Scandinavia. Building on many centuries of glassmaking tradition, Italian designers like Fulvio Bianconi and Ercole Barovier fused pieces of shaped glass into *pezzato* (pieced) vases. This ancient technique was revived by the architect Carlo Scarpa at the Venini glass works in the 1930s. Today, these pieces are highly sought, and a good example can cost as much as a compact car.

RIGHT **Inspired by
Scandinavian designs of the
1950s and 1960s, Jonathan
Adler has created his new
Relief line in natural colors.**
FAR RIGHT ABOVE **More hand-
thrown vessels by Adler, from
the Couture line.**
FAR RIGHT BELOW **A dining table
by John and Sylvia Reid is
laid with American Modern
tableware by Russel Wright.**
OPPOSITE **Rough texturing and
pattern on new and vintage
ceramics. The two balls in the
foreground are lamp bases by
the 1920s French company
Primavera. Behind sits a finger-
streaked 1930s vase by Besnard
and a pot by Adler. The shallow
matte-glazed dish is by Swedish
potter Carl Harry Stålhane.**

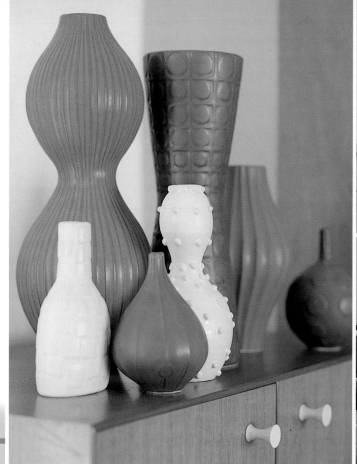

ceramics

**The world of Modern Retro ceramics can encompass anything
from a delicately painted bone-china tea set to an unglazed,
handcrafted earthenware pot. Like glassware, these ceramic pieces
play a multiple role in the home, whether they are used daily,
brought out for special occasions, or permanently on display.**

In the 1920s, the early Modernists took ceramics extremely seriously, seeing them as playing an important role in their program of shaping a new social order through design. Today, pieces by members of the Soviet Constructivist group and the Bauhaus fetch astronomically high prices. However, the bright colors and riotous forms and patterns of ceramic pieces produced by artists like the Russian Kasimir Malevich soon began to influence mass-market ceramic design all around the world, and it is these mass-produced pieces that the Modern Retro homeowner tends to collect and display.

Clarice Cliff, one of the designers from the interwar period whose pieces are most collectable today, was deeply inspired by these radical artists. Bizarre, the name she chose for her line of highly abstracted and colorful pottery, reflected her interest in the anarchic. For many people, the pottery of Clarice Cliff and her contemporary Susie Cooper epitomizes the Art Deco

style. Both designers, extremely popular in their time, predictably fell from fashion in the postwar years and returned to public notice around the early 1970s with the renewed interest in their period. Today their work is highly prized, but some pieces are still affordable.

Equally popular, if not more so, are the simple shapes, sharp angles, and cool colors of the ceramics designed by celebrated potters such as the New Zealander Keith Murray for Wedgwood and the American Frederick Rhead, best known for his very collectable Fiestaware. In the United States and Canada, the work of Russel Wright and Eva Zeisel was the epitome of the Modern Retro look. The styles of both of them are characterized by graceful, sinuous, and asymmetrical shapes that broke away from the circular tyranny of the potter's wheel. From the late 1930s to the early 1960s, Wright's American Modern line and Zeisel's Town and Country dinnerware were the preferred table settings for progressive buyers, as they are today.

But these were patternless designs, and much of the market enjoys decoration. In England in the early 1950s, Roy Midwinter began to produce a line of tableware with designs by Jessie Tait and the young Terence Conran. The names of the patterns were reflections of what it was to be Modern at the time, a

IN ENGLAND IN THE EARLY 1950s, ROY MIDWINTER BEGAN TO PRODUCE TABLEWARE WITH DESIGNS BY JESSIE TAIT AND TERENCE CONRAN. THE NAMES OF THE PATTERNS WERE REFLECTIONS OF WHAT IT WAS TO BE MODERN AT THE TIME, A MIXTURE OF THE EXOTIC AND THE SPACE AGE.

mixture of the exotic and the space age: Galaxy, Tropicana, Nature Study, Patio, Zambesi. However, as with so much of the very best design of the postwar years, it was the Scandinavians who led the field. The Swedish potter Stig Lindberg, working for the firm of Gustavsberg, produced Zeisel-influenced vases as well as whimsical earthenware vessels and tableware decorated with naturalistic but stylized motifs.

The 1940s to the 1960s were also the prime years of several outstanding studio potters. A giant not only in ceramics, who cast his shadow over the whole art world during the first three-quarters of the twentieth century, was the Spanish artist Pablo Picasso. In the mid-1940s, Picasso began working in ceramics, producing a stream of plates and pots that went into serial production. With humorous faces or shaped like strange

birds of unknown species, Picasso's ceramics helped to move pottery from an everyday item to a high art form. Meanwhile, studio potters like Bernard Leach, Hans Coper, Lucie Rie, and Gertrud Vasegaard looked to the long ceramic traditions of Japan and China for inspiration.

In the late 1960s and 1970s attempts were made to shatter this fragile world of good taste. Ettore Sottsass, the *enfant terrible* of the Radical Design movement, began to play with ceramics, giving his pieces blocky, angular forms that were loosely based on the Art Deco revival and kitsch elements from the 1950s. Eventually this led Sottsass and his followers into creating ceramics in the frankly awkward shapes associated with Postmodernism.

CLOCKWISE FROM OPPOSITE ABOVE LEFT **Retro and modern pots side by side; Glazes and forms inspired by Oriental examples; German porcelain—the tall orange demitasses by Schmid and the pierced bowl from the Berlin factory; A collection of ceramic forms in solid colors; Nature Study by Terence Conran for Midwinter in 1955; Zambesi and Tonga, two Jessie Tait patterns for Midwinter; A 1950s stoneware bowl by Gunnar Nyland; A collection of Poole Pottery by Alfred Burgess Read.**

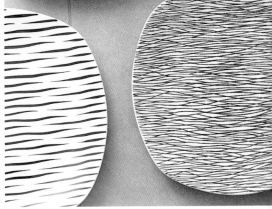

THIS PAGE **Fish- and sharkskin was a very chic covering for ladies' toiletry accessories in the 1920s. These attenuated vases, designed by R & Y Augusti, are made from this scaley-textured material. They stand on a table, the edge inlaid with toothed marquetry, attributed to Ruhlmann.**

LEFT **Grained woods mingled with gloss and matte glazings.**
BELOW LEFT **A hand-turned salad bowl designed by Russel Wright for the Oceana line of 1935.**
BELOW **Collecting is about detail, desire, and knowledge. Upon a pedestal table inspired by Saarinen, and made by Arkana of Bath, is a later edition Ericofon that has more angular edges than the curved form of the earlier line.**

In a Modern Retro interior, there are many objects other than the obvious things like furniture and lighting that impart a period feel. These pieces can range from household appliances, such as the television set looking like a giant white bubble sitting prominently in the corner of the living area, to quirky collectables like cardboard coat hangers shaped in the profiles of John, Paul, George, and Ringo.

A clock that was designed and manufactured only last year is perfectly acceptable in a Modern Retro kitchen, because this style happily mixes the new with the old. However, there is something even more satisfying about seeing a George Nelson clock from the late 1940s, with its spiky face and elegantly shaped hands, hanging above a chrome-legged table and matching vinyl-backed chairs from the same period.

Many original Modern Retro accessories are highly sought collectables, although re-issues of old favorites also allow enthusiasts to purchase pieces that might otherwise be outside their budget. Design shops specializing in Modern re-editions continue to sell, for example, Piero Fornasetti ceramics such as his Architectura coffee set of the 1960s. These re-issues are generally affordable, whereas out-of-production Fornasetti pieces must be acquired through specialized dealers or at auction, and can be extremely expensive.

Life is about those extra-special details. Accessories range from the everyday to the unique, from household appliances to quirky collectables. The Modern Retro interior is their ideal setting.

accessories

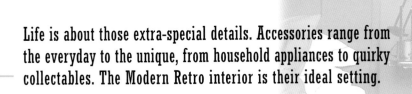

OPPOSITE PAGE RIGHT **A chair designed by Jens Risom for Knoll Furniture around the Second World War is paired with a contemporary Spool clock by George Nelson.** OPPOSITE ABOVE LEFT **The space-age styling of the JVC Videosphere TV is reminiscent of an astronaut's helmet.** OPPOSITE BELOW LEFT **A group of American flea-market finds.**

In auction catalogs of sales of modern design, or in galleries selling collectable Modern pieces, side by side with the higher priced works sit many inexpensive yet beautiful examples of Modernism. These pieces may have been designed by anonymous makers or manufactured by companies that have not become recognized internationally but which nevertheless produced extremely representative pieces of the period.

IN AUCTION CATALOGS OR IN GALLERIES SELLING MODERN PIECES, SIDE BY SIDE WITH THE HIGHER PRICED WORKS SIT MANY INEXPENSIVE YET BEAUTIFUL EXAMPLES OF MODERNISM.

ABOVE LEFT **Dating from the mid-1950s, this George Nelson jewelry chest of rich walnut and plastic laminate sits atop an enameled steel pedestal base. The elegant lamp beside the alarm clock and unusual telephone is a Visor by Arne Jacobsen from the same period.** ABOVE RIGHT **A magazine rack was an essential accessory in every well-furnished living room during the 1950s. This rack is an inexpensive but fun metal example** LEFT **A white plastic flip digital clock and a perspex sculpture by Vasser create a Modern Retro still life on a crowded windowsill.**

Each country has their unknown designers, men and women whose works are familiar within national borders, but whose reputations have not spread beyond. This is the time to pick up pieces by lesser-known designers, before a public gallery or museum holds an exhibition of their work and the prices suddenly soar.

Conversely, some items by established designers are still usable, but most people would rather have them in an up-to-date form. Electrical appliances are a perfect example, telephones in particular. The telephone has a highly respectable design history, and each model says much about the period it represents. The perfect complement to a Modern Retro interior with a

BELOW In postwar France, coat racks such as this one seemed always to be designed with an element of fun about them.

RIGHT No doubt the inspiration for the French coat rack shown below was the famous Hang-It-All by Charles and Ray Eames, a colourful wall-mounted design created for children's rooms for hanging all sorts of things on. The Hang-It-All first sold between 1953 and 1961, and is now available as a re-edition.

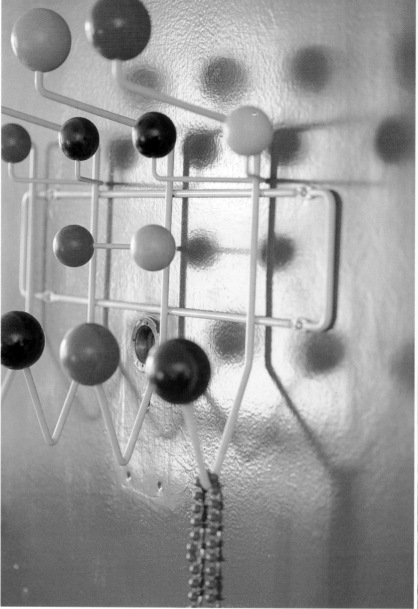

1930s feel is the black Bakelite telephone created by the Norwegian Jean Heiberg for the Swedish company Ericsson and used throughout Scandinavia, Great Britain, and her empire. The 500 telephone from 1950 and the Trimline from 1965, both designed by the great American industrial designer Henry Dreyfuss, became standard in almost every home in the United States. And there is nothing more fun than dialing the bottom of the Ericofon, the world's first one-piece telephone, designed in 1954, which looks like the head of a cobra rearing to strike. Of course, using such telephones today means abandoning certain modern communication

RIGHT A 1960s homage to plastic. The Italian table, designed by M. Siard, has a built-in lamp along the back of the top shelf. The vintage Trimphone was the first push-button telephone. The ball clock is a very fine example made by Presta. Leaning against the wall is a plastic panel by Joe Tilson, one of a series that formed an art wall in the British Pavilion at Expo '67 in Montreal.

facilities such as touch-tone dialling and memory recall, but old phones are often used as second telephones in the Modern Retro home.

The list of collectable accessories is endless. They include leaf-patterned Norwegian serving plates and orange Dansk casserole dishes and a set of flatware by Grethe Meyer in the dining room, a mirror in the hall in the shape of an elephant's head by a wild Pop designer, a Portuguese poster advertising the film *Ben Hur* hanging over the desk in the study, period copies of *House Beautiful* in the wire magazine rack in the living area, and an early transistor radio designed by Dieter Rams on the kitchen work surface. As that great Modernist Mies van der Rohe said, "God is in the details."

THE LIST OF COLLECTABLE ACCESSORIES IS ENDLESS. THEY RANGE FROM LEAF-PATTERNED NORWEGIAN SERVING PLATES AND ORANGE DANSK CASSEROLE DISHES TO A MIRROR IN THE HALL IN THE SHAPE OF AN ELEPHANT'S HEAD BY A WILD POP DESIGNER.

RIGHT **A pair of folding Plia plastic chairs, designed in 1969 by Giancarlo Piretti for Castelli, have become the perfect extra chairs to have about the house. They are easily stored, being very lightweight and made to fold flat to a thickness of only about a single inch. Dating from around the same time are the deep purple plastic bubble wall-hangings by Danish designer Verner Panton. It is believed that these panels were originally created as part of a series destined for a discotheque that was never actually constructed. Panton also created similarly shaped wall lamp fittings. Each panel was decorated with large, circular half-spheres with the bulbs protruding from the center.**

CREATING the Modern Retro look

An American living room that is thoroughly Modern Retro. Two
matching Arne Jacobsen Egg chairs, both with ottomans, are grouped
with a curving sofa and coffee table by Vladimir Kagan. The floor
lights are contemporary, as is the Judy Ross carpet.

Although incredibly diverse in appearance, Modern Retro homes emanate a unity of purpose. Their rooms use furniture and objects designed in the Modern period to create comfortable contemporary interiors. There is no striving after historic room settings—the Modern Retro look is not about museum-style interiors—although some pieces may be of museum quality. Modern Retro interiors can be found in all kinds of houses and apartments, from grand eighteenth-century Paris buildings to converted New York warehouses. Their owners are not slaves to the Modern period that they love, but they know how to use it to create a fresh and individual look.

The living room usually displays the largest collection in the home of the Retro style because some of the best mid-century Modern pieces are chairs, sofas, and coffee tables. Modern Retro delights in combining authentic pieces with re-editions of the works of classic twentieth-century masters and items by today's best designers.

living rooms

The design of the house as we know it today began to evolve during the first thirty years of the twentieth century. World War I was a catalyst for enormous social change, and it was a time when the pioneering architects and designers of the Modern Movement began to rethink the home exterior and interior. By the 1930s, the traditional configuration of the home was undergoing a transformation. Houses were becoming smaller and thus easier to maintain without an army of servants. Instead of being situated on the ground floor, living rooms often occupied a lighter, brighter space on the second floor. Le Corbusier wrote, "The reception-rooms will be at the top, in direct communication with the roof garden, in the fresh air, away from the street with its dust and noise, in full sunshine."

The changes in room usage and styles in this period predominantly followed a course set by the leading names in architecture. One of the earliest Modern interiors that still exerts an influence on today's interiors is the Rietveld Schröder house in Utrecht, Holland, designed by the local architect Gerrit Rietvald in 1924. Although the layout is important for its early multipurpose use of rooms, the innovation of this house lies in the strong use of color, which was influenced by the work of De Stijl artists like Mondrian.

LEFT **American visitors in a London house designed by John Winter: the crisp lines of a Florence Knoll sofa by Knoll International of New York, and three armchairs by Charles and Ray Eames, all 1950s classics. The table is contemporary, an updated redesign of a 1930s rounded shape with two tiers.**

No building or furniture materials were left exposed; all were painted in large blocks of color: red, yellow, blue, white, black, and gray. Horizontal and vertical planes were strongly emphasized. In the 1960s, when big, bold wall graphics were popular, the geometric designs of the surfaces of the Rietveld house hit a resonant chord.

The most influential living rooms of the Modern Movement in the 1920s and 1930s were those created by the purists: Le Corbusier, the Luckhardts, Mies van der Rohe, and Serge Chermayeff. Although their interiors were extremely important, it is evident when examining contemporary photographs of these period houses that they are first and foremost documents of their time, very far removed from the Modern Retro living room.

When in the 1920s and 1930s Modernism began to define itself, designers and architects created a style that one critic of the time, John Gloag, described as suffering from "the Puritan streak." There is a grain of truth in this observation. The interiors shown in old black-and-white and the rare color photographs of the period are austere, uncluttered, almost spartan; devoid of life and people. Yet these are the textbook images for contemporary followers of the Modern

WHEN IN THE 1920s AND 1930s MODERNISM BEGAN TO DEFINE ITSELF, DESIGNERS AND ARCHITECTS CREATED A STYLE THAT ONE CRITIC OF THE TIME, JOHN GLOAG, DESCRIBED AS SUFFERING FROM "THE PURITAN STREAK." THERE IS A GRAIN OF TRUTH IN THIS OBSERVATION.

LEFT The owner of this living room loves to travel and pick up finds along the way. Hence the fine selection of ceramics in this interior, including the French plaster floor lamps from the 1940s. The sofa and matching armchairs are by Ulrich.
RIGHT The graceful wrought-iron frame of a René Pru chair. The round table is a twentieth-century Biedermeier Revival piece.

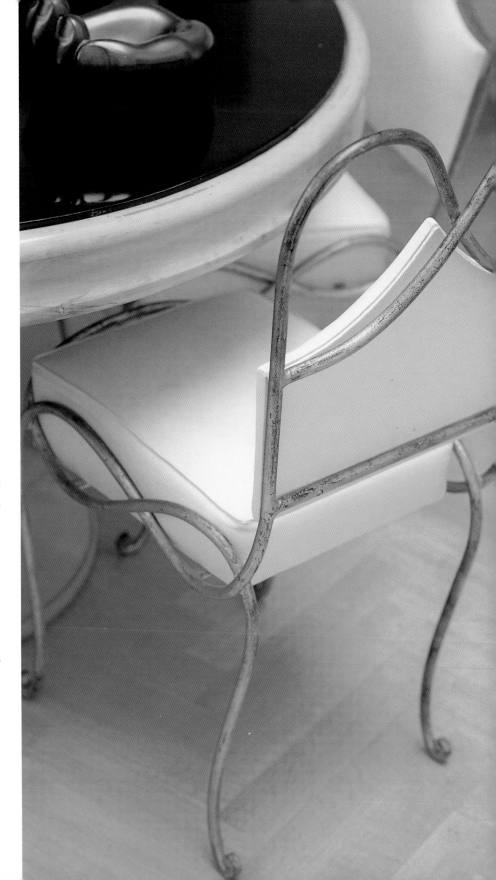

Movement. However, when we strive to recreate the Modernist home in a contemporary interior, we are able to choose the best or most successful elements of Modernism and combine them with up-to-date comforts and other practical developments.

In the United States, Frank Lloyd Wright was an architectural god. No other architect in American history has had such popular appeal. There have been more books written on Wright than on any other twentieth-century architect. People looking for inspiration when it comes to designing and decorating their own homes purchase many of these publications. So, is there such a phenomenon as a Frank Lloyd Wright Retro living room?

Wright designed his first house as early as the 1880s; his last dates from the year he died, 1959. Within this span of time, he developed his own unique look, moving from a heavy Arts and Crafts style to an organic Modernism that was still very reliant upon the values of materials and structure. The most famous example of Frank Lloyd Wright's encounter between man and nature—a legacy of the Arts and Crafts movement—was Fallingwater, the house he designed in 1935 near Bear Run in Pennsylvania. The living room of this exhilarating and extraordinary building feels like the anchor for the whole structure. It juts out over a steep waterfall, yet is firmly embedded in the rock of the hillside. The floor of the living room is gray flagstone, and a great boulder of the cliff face itself protrudes into the room. Large windows with thick wooden frames afford views of the surrounding, heavily wooded landscape. The furnishings, all designed by Wright, are relaxed: a long built-in banquette beneath a ribbon of windows, stools like squashed backless chairs, and sheepskin rugs thrown over tables and sofas.

In the 1960s and 1970s, this vision of rustic clarity received approval from a younger generation wishing to return to nature as part of an alternative lifestyle. The earlier work of Frank Lloyd Wright, whose architecture had fallen out of fashion during the 1950s, enjoyed a burst of new popularity. Suddenly, original furniture designed by Wright was selling for large sums of money. It was soon re-issued by contemporary

**RIGHT An elaborate candelabra replaces a log fire within the bare-brick shell of a fireplace. BELOW RIGHT A little bit of France in England. The living room of this early 1900s house, with its colored glass windows and fine plaster ceiling, is dedicated to mainly French furniture. Surfaces are decorated with the owner's collection of crystal sculpture by Lalique. A neoclassical mirror overlaps the space where an elaborate mantle should be.
OPPOSITE PAGE The legs of these stout armchairs by Leleu seem to buckle under the weight of the upholstery. The glass-topped table in the foreground is by René Drouet. The large mirror by Osvaldo Borsani continues the sinuous lines of the table legs and wall lights.**

ABOVE A tranquil corner of French Art Deco, with a plump stuffed sofa and carpet by Jules-Émile Leleu combined with a little stool, inspired by the sculptures of Brancusi, that doubles as a table.

THIS PAGE **A monumental
column rises through this New
York loft apartment. With no
carpets or rugs to focus
groupings, the furniture
appears to float gently through
the large space. Much of the
furniture is French, including
the Art Deco daybed in an
Empire Revival style.**
OPPOSITE **This 1950s daybed
in a sunny corner was created
by the designer Robsjohn-
Gibbings working for the
Widdicomb Furniture Company
of Grand Rapids, Michigan.**

ABOVE **Two classic English chairs from the 1950s: on the left is a lounger by Robin Day with broad wooden arms for a drink or book; on the right is a broad-backed Flamingo chair by Ernest Race. The biomorphic-shaped occasional table is called Clouds and was designed by Neil Morris of Glasgow in 1947.**
RIGHT **At the center of this room is a large round library table, antique in feel but actually created in the early 1960s by designer Robert Heritage. The console table set against the far wall is another Heritage piece.**

furniture companies who sought to capitalize on the enthusiasm for all things Wright. Indeed, Wright fever is still very much with us today.

The organic Modernism of Frank Lloyd Wright is completely different to the high-society style popular for much of the 1930s, especially as portrayed in Hollywood films of the time. Yet, for many people, the stereotype of the sophisticated Hollywood room set was a far greater influence than any of Wright's designs. Indeed, the film set has continued to fuel the fantasies of many Modern Retro advocates. The studio mogul's luxurious penthouse in the 1939 film *Stage Door* is, for many people, their idea of 1930s interior perfection.

Yet these glossy and glamorous interiors were usually the creations of set designers rather than practising architects, and the results were very similar to the art of the interior designer. It is not surprising therefore that the 1920s and

ABOVE **The maple treads of an open staircase lead down to the spacious living room of a nineteenth-century house in London. The interior is very Modern Retro, setting vintage objects alongside new pieces that have a Retro flavor. An Eames lounge chair and ottoman, that great twentieth-century classic, are coupled with a 1980s sofa and ottoman by British designer Jasper Morrison. On the floor stands a cylindrical lamp, Biproduct, a recent design with a distinct 1970s Retro feel, its body of bright orange with a stainless steel mesh to diffuse the light.**

1930s were the heyday of the interior designer, then still a relatively new profession. Women played leading roles in this world, mainly because the home was so often considered female territory. Fashionable society ladies who wanted to show off their "artistic" skills turned first to decorating for their friends and aquaintances and then, if successful, went into business. Their luxurious style exuded elegance, comfort, and glamour, and was strongly influenced by the Regency period and the neo-Grecian features of the Art Deco look.

One of the most prominent interior decorators of the era was Syrie Maugham, the wife of the well-known author Somerset Maugham. Her most famous creation was the living room in her London home, decorated in 1927 and known as "The White Room" because of its all-white color scheme (*see page 15*). Maugham's long, low sofas, which would not look out of place in one of today's interiors, were upholstered in sleek beige satin; the low occasional and side tables were painted white, and the floor was covered with a huge, specially commissioned rug by Marion Dorn, which was white with a raised geometric pattern. Mirrored

RIGHT **The English furniture designer Robin Day has been called the twentieth-century Chippendale. Much of Day's furniture was made by Hille, such as this fine sideboard from the Hilleplan line of 1952. The pair of side chairs are two years earlier, from the Hillestack line.**
BELOW RIGHT **More Robin Day. The black vinyl on the single convertible settee from 1957 is original. The back is hinged and can be flipped over to create a broad bed.**

THE IMAGE OF THE LIVING ROOM UNDERWENT A CHANGE AFTER WORLD WAR II. THE SPARE INTERIORS OF INTERWAR MODERNISM WERE REPLACED BY A MORE APPROACHABLE STYLE, ONE THAT IS FAMILIAR TO US TODAY. THIS IS BECAUSE MODERNISM BECAME THOROUGHLY AMERICANIZED.

panels lined much of the walls, increasing the overall effect of sophistication. The "all-white" living room was again to became a style statement in the 1970s, in a rejection of the clashing colors and wild effects of 1960s Pop design.

The image of the living room underwent a change after World War II. The spare interiors of interwar Modernism were replaced by a more approachable style, one that is familiar to us today. This is because Modernism became thoroughly Americanized. Superficially, it can be hard to differentiate between a pre- and immediate post-World War II living room when it comes to the furniture and its arrangement. The difference, however, lies in the architectural setting. Early Modernism sought to introduce more space into the interior, but the resulting rooms were a little too hard and austere. What changed, and was to change even more over the following decades, were the textures and varieties of wall and floor coverings, fabrics, and pattern, which made rooms more welcoming and friendly. Americans had introduced the notion of "gracious living."

ABOVE **In another nineteenth-century house, the living space flows through into a dining area. The sofa in the foreground is by Ernest Race, from his DA series designed in the late 1940s; this example has retained its original green upholstery. The chairs and table standing upon a French cowhide are original pieces by the architects John and Sylvia Reid, who are perhaps best known for the progressive lighting designs they produced for the British company Rotaflex during the 1950s. The traditional sideboard remained popular in Britain during this period, and this cherrywood example is another Reid piece.**

THIS PAGE In the living room of this weekend home near the English coast, the look is natural and authentic. When the house was built in the 1930s, the architect Oliver Hill requested that furniture by Alvar Aalto be used in the showhouse. The present owner has obliged. And wood is everywhere: in the wavy lines of the Eames folding screen, the textured relief panel by Brian Willsher, and the spiky lines of the wood sculpture by Antony Twentyman.
OPPOSITE PAGE The Aalto tables, stools, and sideboard on the original pitch pine parquet floor.

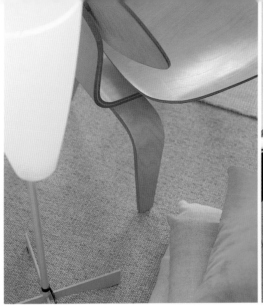

LEFT **The living and dining areas of this house merge effortlessly together and are illuminated by brilliant daylight falling through the tall windows. The all-white theme is heightened by the black surfaces of the Jacobsen Series 7 dining chairs and the Eames surfboard table. Ready for a guest is the broad wooden seat and back of a Lounge Chair Wood (LCW) designed by Charles Eames in 1945-46.**
RIGHT **The feet of the LCW are like those of a ballet dancer on pointes. In similar fashion, the stand of the modern lamp barely seems to be able to balance its towering shade. Much furniture of the postwar era reveled in the engineering feat of balancing awkward loads on skeletal bases.**
FAR RIGHT **The Eames surfboard table is more correctly and practically termed an Elliptical Table Rod Base (ETR).**

For many people who want to create a Modern Retro living room, Philip Johnson's Glass House offers the perfect model. Johnson was responsible for introducing the Modern Movement to the United States with his groundbreaking 1932 exhibition at the Museum of Modern Art in New York. His own house in New Canaan, Connecticut, built in the late 1940s, had a steel frame with exterior walls of glass sheeting. Like its contemporary, the Farnsworth House by Mies van der Rohe, the Glass House is all about transparency. There are no internal dividing walls, only a cylindrical block containing the bathroom and a fireplace.

Like many of the classic Modernist houses of the 1920s and 1930s, the open-plan interior of the Glass House is articulated into room functions by arranging furniture in clear groups. The living area is a case in point. Arranged in a rectangle are a few select pieces of 1930s-designed furniture by Mies van der Rohe: a low couch, two Barcelona chairs, and a stool with, at the center, a glass-topped table. Along one edge of this arrangement, like a screen wall, is a large easel holding a seventeenth-century landscape painting attributed to Poussin. That is all there is to it. The living space of the Glass House was the height of reductionism.

Out of the Glass House and the Farnsworth House grew a movement for designing living spaces that were not only open in plan, like those pioneered before the war, but were also open in terms of transparency and attenuation. Mies van der Rohe's famous statement that "less is more" meant that the living room not only had fewer pieces of furniture in it but also fewer walls. The steel-frame houses built in California in the late 1940s and 1950s did much to explore and popularize this light and airy new way of living. Lifestyle magazines of the period showed handsome young couples in short-sleeved shirts and cotton dresses lounging in their living rooms, the floor-to-ceiling picture

MIES VAN DER ROHE'S FAMOUS STATEMENT THAT "LESS IS MORE" MEANT THAT THE LIVING ROOM NOT ONLY HAD FEWER PIECES OF FURNITURE IN IT BUT ALSO FEWER WALLS. THE STEEL-FRAME HOUSES BUILT IN CALIFORNIA IN THE LATE 1940s AND 1950s DID MUCH TO EXPLORE AND POPULARIZE THIS LIGHT AND AIRY NEW WAY OF LIVING.

LEFT **Rarely does one think of postwar modern furniture as family heirlooms. But the father of the owner of this apartment was an architect, and almost all the furniture in the living area was inherited. The twist in this extremely fine collection takes its cue from the calfhide covering of the Nelson Coconut chair. Several cow skins are also arranged on the floor and thrown over Bertoia Diamond chairs; these coverings were sent by an aunt from Brazil. The aluminum enamel bowls, here grouped on an Eames ETR table, often appeared in high-style interiors of the 1950s. And the lamp is extremely fine, its form like a praying mantis, an extra out of the 1957 horror B-film classic** *The Deadly Mantis.*

windows slid open to create a direct link with the great outdoors. The Stahl House by the architect Pierre Koenig furnished some of the most redolent images of this carefree life. Photographs of the living room taken just after completion in 1960, looking in through the all-glass walls, show elegant women in full skirts and petticoats and debonair men in white tuxedos perched casually on chairs and stools. The living room cantilevers out from the side of the Hollywood Hills. The people and furniture float angelically above the bright lights of Los Angeles—an aspirational scene of glamour and sophistication.

ABOVE **This space doubles as living and sleeping quarters; the built-in sofa converts to a bed. When this small London house was built in the early 1960s, this room was originally part of the kitchen-dining area, an unusual arrangement because it was on the upper floor. However, new owners were able to add a kitchen extension downstairs and convert this room.** .

As early as 1956, a pioneering design exhibition in London looked forward to the trends in living spaces that were to develop during the late 1960s and 1970s. The House of the Future by the British architects Alison and Peter Smithson had much in common with the science-fiction fantasies of the 1950s. Entering through a space pod-type opening, visitors found themselves in "encapsulating spaces" appointed with furniture that could be pushed around on trolley wheels and chairs molded of plastic into orbital shapes. This extreme use of plastic may have seemed avant garde in the mid-1950s, but it was soon to became a reality as design went into revolt in the 1960s. Soon, almost every item in the living room could be made of plastic: chairs, sofas, tables, lights, sideboards, televisions and radios, flower vases. And what a mouthful the names of these plastics were: polyester, polypropylene, polyvinyl chloride (pvc), polyurethane. These were new materials that could be shaped into organic forms or cut with sharp-edged precision.

THIS EXTREME USE OF PLASTIC MAY HAVE SEEMED AVANT GARDE IN THE MID-1950s, BUT IT WAS SOON TO BECOME A REALITY AS DESIGN WENT INTO REVOLT IN THE 1960s. SOON, ALMOST EVERY ITEM IN THE LIVING ROOM COULD BE MADE OF PLASTIC.

ABOVE **The living area of this New York apartment has two seating spaces. This is the more intimate of the two, with the curvy forms of a Noguchi sofa, chairs by Arne Jacobsen and Pierre Paulin, and an asymmetrically shaped rug.**
RIGHT **The alternative seating area in the same apartment. Two Hoffman sofas square each other off across Robsjohn-Gibbings' Mesa table.**

RADICAL DESIGNERS BEGAN TO CREATE ROOM ENVIRONMENTS THAT COULD BE PURCHASED AS DIFFERENT UNITS. THE UNITS COULD BE INTERCHANGED AND REARRANGED, IN KEEPING WITH THE CONTEMPORARY IDEOLOGY OF AN ADAPTABLE LIVING SPACE.

Although the traditional seating arrangement of a sofa, two or more chairs, and a coffee table remained the typical grouping in the living room during the 1960s and 1970s, it was also the period when this part of the house could be described as "an environment." This usually took the form of a closed-in, intimate, but communal world, one that was in direct opposition to the open and transparent style of living espoused by Philip Johnson in the Glass House. The island unit was an example of such an isolated setting at its simplest: usually a large mattress edged with units containing stereo equipment, records, a bar, a telephone, and a television set— anything that could make the zone more relaxing and self-contained. The next step was the sunken seating well, taking the form of built-in banquettes dropped around the edges of a lowered area in the middle of the living room. Sometimes the whole sunken area was carpeted and cushioned, the overall effect being one of a soft and womblike enclosure. In the 1968 film *Barbarella*, Jane Fonda lived and traveled in just such an enclosed environment: a small spaceship with an interior that was completely clad in shagpile carpet; the controls and other equipment were sunk into the floor and raised in shiny plastic bubbles.

Radical designers began to create whole room environments that could be purchased as different units. The units could be endlessly interchanged and rearranged, in keeping with the contemporary ideology of an adaptable living space. Luigi Colani, for example, created his Pool Living Pad in the early 1970s. This was simply a series of foam blocks, each one about 30 inches square, covered in fabric and laid side by side to make a soft raised surface. Here one could lounge, watch TV, read, or sleep. Stretching from wall to wall, it made for a furniture-less living room.

LEFT **Collecting just what you like sometimes makes for a cumulative and eclectic look, as in this living area. One very good piece is Pillola, the mini Oldenburg-inspired capsule pill lamp perched at the left end of the mantelpiece. Designed by Cesare Casati and Emanuele Ponzio in 1968, this piece can be considered tangentially as a fun piece of Pop Art and a dissonant statement made by late 1960s counterculturists in Italian design, the Radical Group.**

The ever-versatile and imaginative Danish designer Verner Panton reversed the idea of a sunken living space. One of his early ideas was to suspend seating from the ceiling on wires. Then, in the late 1960s, he introduced his Pantower: sofalike units with cutout shapes that could be stacked up in various configurations for sitting and lying on in several different positions. The design historian Lesley Jackson has remarked that commentators of the period described the Pantower as a "living room honeycomb."

OPPOSITE **In a 1970s London high-rise, the original kitchen design and fixtures have been retained. Natural light from the extensive sheetglass window situated high in the sky flows into this compressed but articulately arranged kitchen. Plush, comfortable dining is possible with a 1920s two-seater sofa.**

LEFT **A Robin Day orchestra chair from the Royal Festival Hall of 1951 is tucked beneath a patterned laminate-top table by Frank Guille.**

RIGHT **Pictures, furniture, and objects make this setting intensely abstract, individual, and aesthetically Modern.**

In Germany during the mid-1920s, Bauhaus architects took up the lessons learned from the American domestic economist Christine Frederick. They developed her initial idea, one that was of great importance in kitchen design and has grown to become the norm in almost every home—the built-in kitchen. For centuries, the kitchens of the comfortable classes in society had been a conglomeration of individual pieces of furniture, each fulfilling a different function—the cooking range, hutch, and chopping block, to name a few. In many households there were rooms for separate functions—a pantry, a larder, and a scullery, for example. The Modern Movement brought all these elements together into one room, and for convenience into one near-single and unbroken unit.

During the 1930s, the Germans were responsible for calculating, with precise scientific rationalism, every position of the body when moving about the kitchen preparing a meal. How far does the average person stretch to reach for a can on the top shelf? How much area is required to open the oven door? With a multitude of new facts and figures at their fingertips, designers

kitchens and dining rooms

Some of the earliest and most innovative ideas on modern kitchen design originated from the Bauhaus in the mid-1920s. Functionalism was a key tenet at this pioneering school of design, and as the kitchen demanded practicality and efficiency more than any other space in the house, it was the room that received the most rigorous attention and treatment.

planned new kitchens and standardized the size of kitchen units. Today's mass-produced kitchens, built from a selection of modular units that fit together in an unlimited but unified manner, have their origins in these early studies of the Modern Movement.

The kitchens of the Bauhaus are a little too austere for contemporary tastes. They look too much like laboratories, sterile and clinical. However, Grete Schütte-Lihotzky's "Frankfurt kitchen" of 1926, which she designed for minimal apartments, has recently received much attention and prompted renewed

TODAY'S MASS-PRODUCED KITCHENS, BUILT FROM A SELECTION OF MODULAR UNITS, HAVE THEIR ORIGINS IN THE STUDIES OF THE MODERN MOVEMENT.

interest in this early Modern architect's conviction that as much kitchen work as possible should be done sitting down. The result is new kitchens with more leg room under the work surfaces.

In the 1930s and 1940s, American companies first began to mass-produce the double layer of horizontal cabinets that were to become standard kitchen design in the following decades. These "built-in" kitchens had a row of wall cupboards that ran overhead, paralled by a row of enclosed cabinets below. Kitchen plans became uniform, with four typical layouts: the single strip, the double galley, the U- and L-shapes. The entire approach to kitchen design became more scientific. Appliances underwent a transformation, with industrial designers such as

ABOVE LEFT **The immaculate Danish Modernism of designer Nanna Ditzel.**

ABOVE **The colors for this new kitchen in a 1970s Span house in London were inspired by the kitchen in the house designed by architect Richard Rogers for his parents in 1968. The black laminate surface sets off the orange laminate splashback and the greens of the units and Jacobsen Series 7 chairs.**

RIGHT **More Series 7 chairs, these ones with a natural finish, set around a specially commissioned kitchen table with a sturdy wooden column supporting a granite top.**

THIS PAGE AND OPPOSITE **In a spacious kitchen, a handsome set of Cherner chairs by Paul Goldman encircles a matching table. Two versions of the chair are included in this collection, one with the ribbon arms made from a single strip of walnut-faced molded plywood, the other without. The Cherner chair was designed in 1957.**

LEFT **A vertical acrylic
sculpture by Vasser brings a
slender stroke of color into
this small New York kitchen.
The owner is fascinated by
circular shapes, as exemplified
by the marble-topped pedestal
table by Eero Saarinen and the
round mosaic tiles of the built-
in kitchen unit.**
THIS PAGE **These circular tiles
are more usually associated
with floors and bathrooms, but
work effectively in the kitchen.**

ABOVE CENTRE **At a kitchen nook stands a pair of tall breakfast stools with little laminated beech back rests by Frank Guille.**
ABOVE RIGHT **A white dining room gets a bold injection of color from a vibrant orange rug, the blue covering of the aluminum BA chairs, and the light plywood finish of the delicate little Unicorn stacking chair, both by Ernest Race.**

Norman Bel Geddes streamlining and reshaping kitchen equipment to make it less cumbersome and more appealing. The stove or oven, which had traditionally been made of heavy black cast-iron, metamorphosed to become lighter in weight and color. The new stoves were white-enameled to create a hygienic effect and coordinated in height and depth with the base units of the rest of the kitchen. Large refrigerators, fitted with every possible gadget, became the norm. In the U.S. in particular, appliance design was greatly influenced by contemporary automobile design, a fact that is reflected in their streamlined shapes and styling details.

Today it is still possible to find retro stoves and have them reconditioned, thus obtaining a period feel while still meeting today's household demands. And old fridges can, once over-hauled, still hum efficiently and quietly in the modern kitchen. Alternatively, modern retro-style refrigerators, especially those mimicking the old streamlined Fridgidaires of the 1950s, with their squat broad bodies and rounded edges, have made a great comeback recently and are now available in many appliance and department stores.

Since the 1930s, kitchens have slowly taken on more personality. The utilitarian kitchens of the past, run by servants, were considered "service quarters" and strictly places of business. But as household help became harder to find after World War I, mothers in traditional middle-class families began to take up the role formerly played by servants. The kitchen became a woman's territory, an extension of female domesticity and the heart of family life.

DINING BECAME MORE INFORMAL. EATING SPACES WERE COMBINED WITH KITCHEN FIXTURES, AND A "BREAKFAST NOOK," PERHAPS WITH MATCHING BANQUETTES, WAS OFTEN INCLUDED.

Dining became more informal. Eating spaces were combined with kitchen fixtures, and a "breakfast nook," perhaps with banquettes, was often included. The breakfast bar was another favorite feature. By the mid-1950s, island counters in the middle of the kitchen became popular. Sometimes these island units had gas or electric burners built in. Kitchen barbecueing also became a great fad, particularly if you lived in a wet or northern climate, and large open grills were a fashionable feature of many 1950s and 1960s kitchens, allowing the fun of outdoor cooking to be brought inside. Sometimes indoor barbecues imitated the big rough-brick ovens in the backyard; other times, in the more elegant kitchen, a simple broiler with an electric spit was enough.

In the postwar years, cooking and entertaining at home became enormously popular. Serious cookbook writers such as Elizabeth David and James Beard were followed by a new generation of television cooks like Graham Kerr, the Galloping Gourmet. Kitchens of the 1960s and 1970s became mini-restaurants, equipped with

OPPOSITE PAGE **In this New York loft, an exposed service duct runs along the ceiling parallel to the dining table below. The molded plywood Jacobsen Series 7 chairs are a natural wood finish. The table, with its integrated candleholders, was specially commissioned from the architectural practice The Moderns. The distinctive paper shade is by Noguchi.**
ABOVE LEFT **Deep red lines of painted wall cut horizontal bars across Nanna Ditzel's dining area. The Trinidad chairs are her own design.**
LEFT **This dining area in a New York apartment doubles as a library. The table and chairs are by Charlotte Perriand.**

a *batterie de cuisine* and every accessory. But, by the late 1960s and early 1970s, women began to be liberated and kitchens emancipated. Wives no longer stayed at home all day; they went out to work. And, significantly, more people began to live alone. Soon the kitchen became less a gourmet showcase and better adapted to busier and more peripatetic lifestyles, with a hasty breakfast grabbed in the morning and a quick dinner late at night.

By the end of the 1970s, a look called "the futuristic kitchen" was jokingly invented. This was not the place for the serious cook or the dedicated gourmet. Dominated by the microwave oven and freezer, the room had colors and decorations as fantastic as the gadgets. Surfaces were shiny and metal, sleek and plastic, or soft and carpeted. Standard cupboards and cabinets were replaced by interlocking work units and shelves in floor-to-ceiling tubular cupboards. The kitchen began to resemble a cooking capsule on a space station.

ABOVE LEFT **A mirror reflects the squared grid of a glass wall that divides a kitchen and dining area. The lighting is a pair of floor lamps with spun aluminum shades and adjustable settings that date from the mid-1950s and are by British designers John and Sylvia Reid.**
LEFT **In 1970, when the owners moved to this New York apartment, they inherited this vintage kitchen, complete with its original fixtures.**
ABOVE **This extension was added to an existing Modern house to hold the kitchen. The tall architectural radiator is Danish, by Hudevad.**
OPPOSITE **An early 1950s Italian tri-lamp stands like a sculpture beside a commissioned dining set made of laminated surfaces on square steel legs.**

Traditional houses and apartments always had a separate dining room for eating. In the 1920s, dining rooms in the Art Deco style were places of opulent display. But, compared to the lavishness of the Federal and Victorian settings, the Art Deco style was positively pared down, clearly on the path to the uncompromising look of emerging Modernism.

LEFT **In this open-plan 1970s house, the kitchen flows into the dining area. Originally used in office settings, the Eames table on castors and plastic side chairs are today often used in a home setting. Dishwashing is made much more fun with the colorful swan-neck faucet designed by Arne Jacobsen.**
RIGHT **A Mona Lisa triptych by Ed Paschke overlooks a dark and intimate dining room. The chairs are interesting on account of their acrylic frames.**

BELOW **In this dining setting, the two Postmodern high-backed chairs are of particular interest. On the left of the table is a Gaetano Pesce Greene Street chair, while Robert Venturi's Chippendale is on the far side of the table.**

IN THE POSTWAR HOME, AS EATING IN THE KITCHEN BECAME MORE COMMON, THE DINING ROOM WAS RESERVED FOR SPECIAL OCCASIONS.

With the Modern Movement, dining room walls came tumbling down. The new vogue for large open spaces with cells for different functions meant that dining rooms were increasingly arranged as recesses off a central living area. Sliding and folding screens were one means of dividing the two areas—especially useful for hiding the mess of the dining table when moving to the living area for after-dinner coffee. The Modernism of the 1930s, supposedly egalitarian, made less use of servants. However, servants were sometimes concealed rather than eliminated completely. Many early Modern Movement dining areas were divided from the kitchen or serving area by walls with hatches. There was no need for a serving maid; the unseen cook could pass the meals discreetly through the hatch to the dining area.

The dining room has always had connotations of formality. In the postwar home, eating in the kitchen became more common, and the dining area was reserved for Sunday lunch or special occasions. It thus required furniture that was distinctive, and traditional dining-room items such as the sideboard were updated. Most of the major furniture designers of the 1940s and 1950s turned their hands to sideboards. Florence Knoll's rosewood sideboard is an American classic, as is the 1950s sideboard by the British designer Robert Heritage, with a image of a cityscape by his wife Dorothy silkscreened on the doors.

LEFT There is still something Dickensian about high stools, although this seat, Perch, designed by George Nelson in 1964, is a far cry from the days when Bob Cratchet sat hunched over Mr. Scrooge's accounts. ABOVE A work area in a bedroom. If desired, the desk can be completely folded away in the Comprehensive Storage System (CSS), designed by Nelson in the late 1950s.

BELOW When their backs begin to ache after sitting up at the pair of draughtman's boards, the designer owners of this New York apartment can relax on the Florence Knoll sofa.

Work areas and studies are an increasingly common feature of today's homes. In the past, the kitchen table was often pressed into service as a temporary work space. But as the internet links us closer together, many people now work from home and require a specific work space or room. Moreover, our activities and interests often demand a special area for hobbies or household tasks.

Traditionally, the study was a separate room in a home setting and an exclusively male domain—women had dainty boudoirs furnished with pretty writing desks. The study was a room that evolved from a combination of uses, especially as an adjunct to the library, as a writing room, and as an office from which to run the affairs of the house. It was crammed with books, papers, and furniture.

In the 1920s and 1930s, the high Modern Movement vanquished the cluttered study and replaced it with an almost clinical laboratory-type environment. The work room was seen as a space that had much in common with the bathroom and kitchen, and accordingly it was treated

work rooms

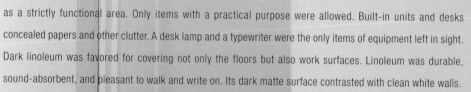

THIS PAGE **A study with a very fine vintage Home Office desk by George Nelson, complete with its leather-covered writing surface. Even the Rolodex is an original period piece.**
ABOVE **Behind the AX chair, by Hvidt and Nielsen, is a draper's shop counter used as a work organizer and filing system.**

as a strictly functional area. Only items with a practical purpose were allowed. Built-in units and desks concealed papers and other clutter. A desk lamp and a typewriter were the only items of equipment left in sight. Dark linoleum was favored for covering not only the floors but also work surfaces. Linoleum was durable, sound-absorbent, and pleasant to walk and write on. Its dark matte surface contrasted with clean white walls.

A 1930s study created by the British architect Rodney Thomas for an apartment in Highpoint I, an ultramodern building in London, was a typical work space of the period, full of optimistic ideals. A built-in work unit made of polished ibus board, which was believed not to warp, lined the walls. The desktop was natural Oregon pine, golden in color to match the cream walls. The unit's corners were gently rounded to prevent them from collecting

dust. The desk section of the unit dropped low in front of the window, and the companion stool had a tubular body. Color was introduced in the form of a giant clock face that dominated almost the whole of one wall: the hour hand was a metal circle painted blue, and the minute hand was bright red. In place of conventional beading, a scarlet silk cord covered the seams in the walls and furniture.

THIS PAGE **An executive's home office. The look is very 1970s, the date of this London apartment, with furniture richly finished in teak and rosewood. The wall coloring is also typical of the period.**

THIS PAGE **A towering stack of plastic storage units by the Bologna-based furniture company Castelli.**
RIGHT **In this New York apartment, a desk from the Eames Storage Unit (ESU) line looks a little like a Mondrian painting set against the zinc surfaces of the flush-fitting closet doors.**

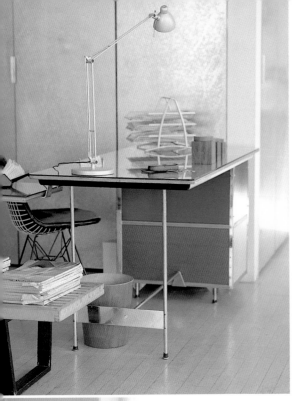

After World War II, the study or work room extended its function to became a place of relaxation and leisure pursuits. Seating areas, sometimes centered around occasional tables, bookshelves, and phonographs for listening to music, often made the rooms less officelike. These new pieces of furniture were low slung, as was the fashion in the 1950s, and thus they were subordinated to the desk, which remained the primary focus of the room.

In houses where space was at a premium, work areas were fitted into a corner of the living room, bedroom, or kitchen. For the housewife, the kitchen was both workshop and office. In the kitchen of the 1950s and early 1960s, the kitchen office, usually a simple desk with a telephone, was a common feature. "The kitchen office is the cook's [i.e. woman's] counterpart of father's den," commented an American publication on kitchens in 1962. "It gives her convenient work space where she can plan her menus, order supplies, neatly record her household expenses—and it could even be used as a space where a young child can draw or read while mother does other work in the kitchen."

In the 1950s, many larger furniture companies began to manufacture office systems that often found their way into the home study. In the 1950s and 1960s, one of the most successful was the Italian manufacturer Olivetti, makers of desks, chairs, office equipment, and, most notably, typewriters. The Valentine portable typewriter designed by Ettore Sottsass and Perry King around 1970 has now become a collector's item.

Today, with the rise of the personal computer, the work space is a practical area where children play computer games and adults do household accounts and surf the internet. There are many excellently designed desks and chairs from the Modern era that can bring an atmosphere of period style to contemporary work rooms.

LEFT **A wooden office–parquet floors, antique table, Jacobsen chair, and a desk with wheels.**
RIGHT **There is a slightly transitory feel about this work space, perhaps because the plywood table with rod legs by Eames folds away after use. The chair, by Saarinen, has been in production since 1948.**

Today the bedroom is another living area of the home. The introduction of the television, video, telephone, and stereo has contributed to the room's expanded function. Whereas the bed is still at the heart of any arrangement, these modern extras, plus typical pieces of furniture such as chairs, closets, and dressing units, offer many opportunities for embracing the Modern Retro look.

The Modernists reacted strongly against the decorative qualities of the turn-of-the-century bedroom. At the Bauhaus exhibition of 1923 in Weimar, Germany, the Sample House had a lady's bedroom furnished by Marcel Breuer. The single bed, made of lemon wood and walnut, had an adorned footboard and a beautifully shaped headboard. A simple rug was thrown on the floor. A chair with a bentwood seat and square back was positioned in front of a dresser with two mirrors: one long and fixed for full-length viewing, the other round and movable for close work. Breuer's bedroom proved very influential, and early Modern Movement houses were quick to adopt this severe, pared-down look.

During the 1920s and 1930s, bedroom furniture was gradually minimized. The structure of bed frames became lighter, as did mattresses when springs replaced heavy mattress stuffing. Beds became lower, giving them less prominence within the room. Heavy bedsteads and tall headboards were banished, as was the ubiquitous marble-topped bedside chest. Smooth surfaces succeeded the ornamental, while sleek veneers replaced solid wood.

The great German Modern Movement architect Eric Mendelsohn furnished his own late 1920s house in Berlin with a guest bedroom that was reminiscent of a train's sleeping compartment. A tubular

ABOVE **By day, the George Nelson bed is kept in the post-war style with a sharp-edged coverlet and severe bolster. The textile is vintage, designed by Estelle Laverne around 1947 and entitled Fun to Run.**

LEFT **This bedroom emanates Zen calm in the middle of crazy New York. Sliding doors with panels of laminated sea grass screen a bed that is raised on a platform and surrounded by plywood-lined walls. The long bench is by Jean Prouvé.**

bedrooms

Bedrooms are places of fantasy, and their furnishing and decoration is a very personal affair. Some people opt for a spirit of tranquility in an attempt to induce restfulness and relaxation, while others choose bright colors and wild patterns to provide a backdrop to unbridled pleasures.

steel-framed bed neatly folded down from a concealed wall space, and the bedside light (a genuine sleeping-compartment lamp) telescoped out from the built-in closets.

After World War II, the Modern bedroom became softer and gentler in appearance. One famous example was the bedroom Philip Johnson redecorated for the use of his guests in 1953. In contrast to the transparent qualities of his Glass House, in New Canaan, Connecticut, Johnson erected a guest house in the yard that was almost impenetrable to the gaze. A small oblong block set away from the main house, the guest wing had only three windows, and these were along the wall that faced away from the principal residence. The main space of the guesthouse was the bedroom, which has become well known not only as a foil to the very exposed bedroom in the Glass House, but also as a room of seductive beauty. The bed was low. There were no bedside tables or lights. All lighting was indirect. The walls were draped completely in pink Fortuny fabric wallhangings, and the ceiling was a series of vaults inspired, according to the architect, by the work of the early nineteenth-century British architect Sir John Soane.

The Johnson guest room had a walk-in closet that was quite separate from the bedroom. This desire to detach sleeping areas from those reserved for dressing and the storage of clothing was an age-old luxury, reminiscent of the grand houses of earlier periods that had a dressing room adjacent to the bedroom. In the Modern period, this separation of functions returned. Some apartments and houses were large enough to accommodate spacious walk-in closets that acted as dressing rooms, but in the majority of cases, built-in armoires had to suffice. The masking of a whole wall by flush closet doors was a typical new feature. Unlike the large freestanding armoires of past centuries that stood so prominently in the room that they all but proclaimed the existence of their contents, the sleek uniformity of the built-in closet hid garments from the mind's eye completely.

It was during the 1950s that the bedroom first began to take on the characteristics of a multifunctional space. Teenagers demanded that their bedrooms become their own preserve. To give the look of a living area, it became common to transform the bed into a divan during the day. Pillows and quilts were removed and put away in closets or chests. Smooth covers were spread over the bed, and a few casually arranged pillows completed the transformation. The addition of a desk or writing table and a chair also assigned the bedroom another role. Work tables, for sewing or hobbies, were other popular additions. Banished forever was the classic free-standing,

ABOVE **A television by Robin Day makes an eccentric bedside table. This model was made by the English company Pye, and dates from 1956. The Nelsonlike slatted bench is also by Robin Day, with black metal rod legs in a V-formation.**

ABOVE **Salvaged hospital furniture—a lamp and a table—are domesticated in a New York bedroom.**
RIGHT **Spot guards his territory. A 1970s bedspread in the style of designer-decorator David Hicks.**

THIS PAGE For the coldest of winter nights, a fun-fur throw lies alongside newly designed pillows by Jonathan Adler. Lighting is provided by a pair of classic 1930s task lamps by Best & Lloyd. Another Nelson bench is positioned at the end of the bed.
LEFT A row of three units, each different and in various woods—oak, teak, rosewood—yet all by George Nelson, as is the bench with wide metal legs.

bulky dresser, with a stationary central mirror and two hinged wings—"rather reminiscent of the triptychs from Gothic altars," according to the design critics Gerd and Ursula Hatje.

Raising furniture off the floor as much as possible gave bedrooms a new, lighter atmosphere. Headboards attached to the bed evolved into long units anchored on to the wall behind the bed. These new headboards were usually not upholstered and sometimes had lighting and side tables built in. Closets too were built in and suspended from the wall and might be left open top and bottom for ventilation. In the mid-1960s, the British furniture makers Hille launched a wall-storage system designed by Alan Turville and John Lewak that hung free of the floor and was advertised with the slogan "Look, no feet!"

In 1961, the Herman Miller company began to manufacture contract storage units designed by Charles Eames. These single systems were attachable to one wall of a bedroom. Used mainly in university dormitories, they typified many of the built-in storage units designed for home use. All the disparate elements of the bedroom were unified into one self-contained unit for sleeping, storage, and working. Storage closets came

RIGHT **A custom-made bed is positioned lengthwise in a non-traditional manner in this New York bedroom, allowing the owner to lie and gaze out of the window over a magnificent view of the Empire State Building. The tubular chrome chair and marble lamp table are interwar pieces. The thin shelves on the walls allow the owner's collection of artworks to be rearranged according to taste.**

IN THE LATE 1960s AND EARLY 1970s, THE BEDROOM BROKE FREE FROM THE CONSTRAINTS OF "GOOD" DESIGN. THE FASHION FOR POP AND OP DESIGN AND THE NOTION OF "LET IT ALL HANG OUT" ENTERED THE BEDROOM AS PART OF THE SEXUAL REVOLUTION.

equipped with wire shelves and drawers, coat hooks, and lights. There was a desk with built-in shelves, a pinboard, and a filing cabinet. The bed could be neatly folded away out of sight during daytime hours.

In the late 1960s and early 1970s, the bedroom broke free from the constraints of "good" design. The fashion for Pop and Op design and the notion of "let it all hang out" entered the bedroom as part of the sexual revolution. The most famous bedroom was that of John Lennon and Yoko Ono, who staged Sleep Ins and Bed Ins in the name of world peace. In the 1960s bedroom, beds were sometimes done away with

d

ABOVE **This child's bedroom looks straight out of the Pop Art period of the late 1960s. The room is full of bold, saturated color—vivid tangerine walls, a lipstick-pink bedspread by the celebrated Finnish textile manufacturer Marimekko, and a lemon-yellow George Nelson bedside table. The concept of the giant alphabet letter as wall ornament was a Pop fashion.**

RIGHT **A luxurious slippery silk throw is cast over an inviting double bed that ends in a George Nelson bench.**

and replaced by mattresses on the floor. Brightly patterned Indian cotton bedspreads added an exotic touch, and the Japanese futon made its first appearance in the West.

The one-room-living approach appealed to designers like Joe Colombo. In 1969 he created a "central living block." This was a raised square of flat interlocking cushions for sitting and reclining. In the center was a bar and overhead a revolving bookcase and television set. Attached was a "night cell block," a space for sleeping. A similar idea was shown in Terence Conran's 1974 manual *The House Book*. A picture in the bedrooms section shows a semiclad couple reclining on a large red plush-velvet-covered island bed with a built-in stereo system. He sips a glass of red wine, staring longingly at a scantily-clad blonde, who in turn gazes up at the overhead slide projection of an erotic Helmut Newton photograph.

It is of course an irony, that for all the care taken in the decoration of the Modern Retro bedroom, this is the place where we spend one third of our lives unconscious.

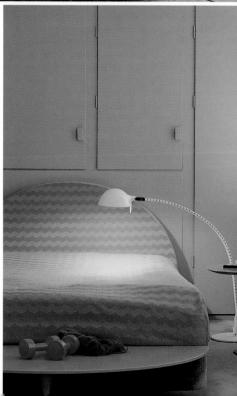

THIS PAGE **A steely-blue bedroom with a pair of Richard Sapper Tizio lamps and a huge wall-mounted speaker in one corner contributing to the High-tech feel.**
BELOW LEFT **A brave use of colors in this superbly elegant and highly finished bedroom setting by Danish designer Nanna Ditzel.**

For many people in the early twentieth century, Modernism began in the bathroom. This utilitarian and functional room was one that wholeheartedly lent itself to the love of practicality and the pared-down aesthetic that were so characteristic of the Modern Movement.

bathrooms

At the beginning of the nineteenth century, the bathroom as a distinct room in the house did not exist—the toilet was outside, and people washed in a tin tub with water heated on the range or fire. The industrious Victorians, however, raised the standards of personal hygiene to a level unknown in history outside the great baths of Rome, and by the late nineteenth century many wealthy homes had bathrooms. The furnishings in these bathrooms were mainly movable: a washstand (a small table with a bowl and pitcher), a free-standing cast-iron bathtub, and a chamber pot concealed in an enclosed chair.

By the 1920s, bathrooms had permanent sanitary fixtures, such as a pedestal-based sink and a neatly boxed-in bathtub. The fixtures were usually sparkling and hygienic, made of white vitreous china. These developments had been assisted by the introduction of new technology such as plumbing for hot and cold water.

The idea of tiling in the bathroom was a nineteenth-century obsession, but in the 1920s and 1930s, bathroom tiling reached new standards. The executive bathroom designed for the wealthy property developer Irwin Chenin set the look for mainstream bathrooms of the period. Situated on the 52nd floor of Chenin's famous Art Deco skyscraper in New York City, the bathroom was designed by the Frenchman Jacques Delamare in the late 1920s. The effect was that of a golden sunset. Wall tiles shaped like rivulets shimmered in gold and cream. The bathtub was enclosed by glass shower doors engraved with a pattern of triangles and quarter-circles. Over these doors there was a ventilating fanlight made of bronze in a sunray pattern.

RIGHT **Finding an apartment or house with its original bathroom intact is a gift. This is a fine example from the early years of the twentieth century, complete with wall tiles that imitate brick facing. The 1950s Bird chair is by Harry Bertoia.**

THIS PAGE **The conversion of an existing room of a house or apartment into a bathroom allows for large open windows and plenty of space—features not usually associated with this part of the home. The Butterfly stool by Sori Yanagi, first produced in 1956, adds something of the flavor of the Japanese bathhouse.**
RIGHT **An original 1920s bathroom with a dowelled slatted-back chair by Paul McCobb from the 1950s.**

In the early 1930s, two enormously influential but very different bathrooms appeared. The first one, designed along traditional lines, has sadly disappeared. The second, powerfully Modern in style, is still admired by thousands of visitors every year.

Following in the tradition of the Chenin bathroom was a bathroom designed by the artist Paul Nash in 1932 for the dancer Tilly Losch and installed in the eighteenth-century London townhouse of her husband, the great Surrealist collector Edward James. The walls of the bathroom were lined with stippled silver glass interlocked with sheets of pink-tinted mirror glass. On the ceiling was a large oblong mirror, edged with fluorescent lights, while half-moon-shaped tubular lights shone from the walls. The fixtures were made of chrome and included, appropriately enough for a dancer, a practice barre.

The second important and influential bathroom from this period is one designed around 1930 by the architect Le Corbusier for the Villa Savoye, just outside Paris. Three of the bathroom walls are tiled white, while the fourth wall is a curtain attached to a pole that provides privacy from the master bedroom.

LEFT Some pieces of disposable furniture from the Pop era still survive. In this bathroom stands the flowering form of an original Tomotom chair, made of cardboard, and designed in the late 1960s by Bernard Holdaway for Hull Traders.

BELOW In a New York bathroom, with a vintage sink and aluminum 1950s lamp, the theme is the sea, and especially sponges from the class *Porifera*, as the large and instructive poster points out.

The bathtub is a sunken rectangle, lined with turquoise ceramic tiles that also cover much of the bathroom floor. Beside the curtain partition is one of the famous features of the Villa Savoye, a concrete reclining bed tiled in gray molten glass. Its sinuous curve evokes the chaise longue designed a few years earlier by Le Corbusier and Charlotte Perriand; the other inspiration was the architect's visit to Turkish baths in the Middle East.

Many of the same hygienic standards that apply to the kitchen are also relevant in the bathroom. In terms of fixtures and materials, the Modern period adopted a similar approach to both rooms. In the 1940s and 1950s, new easy-to-clean plastic laminates became standard finishes in both kitchens and bathrooms. Built-in cabinets were covered in brightly colored and patterned Formica or Warerite surfaces: the top in one color, the drawers in another, and the body in a third. Vinyl wallpapers, supposedly resistant to the problem of bathroom condensation, were also used in kitchens.

From the 1930s on, bathtubs, sinks, and toilets became available in a variety of colors, and it was possible to buy a color-coordinated set. Bathtubs became lighter in weight as new materials like fiberglass and acrylic entered the market.

As the decades progressed, the bathroom became less antiseptic and more comfortable, sometimes a cross between a living room and a bedroom. Floors were carpeted or covered with cork tiles, and large rooms in older houses were converted into bathrooms with the bathtub in the middle of the room and chairs and sofas around the edges. The single light fixture overhead was abandoned for subtle concealed lighting. Saunas and jacuzzis were integrated. The bathroom had gone from a private chamber to a communal space.

THE SECOND IMPORTANT AND INFLUENTIAL BATHROOM FROM THIS PERIOD IS ONE DESIGNED AROUND 1930 BY THE ARCHITECT LE CORBUSIER FOR THE VILLA SAVOYE, JUST OUTSIDE PARIS.

Source directory

Jonathan Adler
465 Broome Street
New York
NY 10012
212-941-8950
A collection of contemporary ceramics with
a Retro sensibility.

Aqua
1415 South Congress
Austin
TX 78704
512-916-8800
Twentieth-century modern lighting and
furniture.

Artemide
46 Greene Street
New York
NY 10012
212-925-1588
The Italian manufacturer of many
contemporary lighting classics, including
Richard Sapper's Tizio.

B & B Italia
800-872-1697
Understated Italian furniture with a strong
contemporary look. Call for details of
stockists nationwide.

Boomerang For Modern
2040 India Street
San Diego
CA 92101
619-239-2040
Twentieth-century modern design.

Cassina USA
155 East 56th Street
New York
NY 10022
800-770-3568
This Italian manufacturer produces re-
issues of many of this century's most
classic pieces of furniture, such as Gerrit
Rietveld's Red/Blue chair and many Le
Corbusier pieces. Call for details of
stockists nationwide.

Chartreuse International
711 East Pike
Seattle
WA 98122
206-328-4844
Twentieth-century classics by Charles and
Ray Eames, Isamu Noguchi, Arne Jacobsen,
and others.

Cherry
185 Orchard Street
New York
NY 10012
212-358-7131
Modern furnishings and accessories.

Circa 50
www.circa50.com
This website offers furniture by Charles and
Ray Eames, Verner Panton, Arne Jacobsen,
Isamu Noguchi, and Ernest Race, as well as
tableware by American ceramicists Russel
Wright and Eva Zeisel.

Design within Reach
455 Jackson Street
San Francisco
CA 94111
800-944-2233
www.dwr.com
Order modern classics from their online
showroom.

Donzella
17 White Street
New York
NY 10013
212-965-8919
A collection of vintage pieces.

Form and Function
95 Vandam Street
New York
NY 10013
212-414-1800
www.formandfunctiondesign.com
Vintage furniture and lighting design from
1945–1975. Also electronics, ceramics,
jewelry, and accessories.

Full House
38 Renwick Street
New York
NY 10013
646-486-4151
Vintage pieces.

Full Upright Position
1200 NW Everett
Portland
OR 97209
800-431-5134
www.f-u-p.com
Modern classics for sale on the internet.
Call for a catalog.

Good Eye
4918 Wisconsin Avenue NW
Washington
DC 20016
202-244-8516
www.goodeyeonline.com
Vintage lighting, decorative objects, textiles,
and housewares from designers including
Robsjohn-Gibbings, Russel Wright, Arne
Jacobsen, and Harry Bertoia.

Inform
97 Water Street
Vancouver, B. C.
Canada
604-682-3868
Re-editions of modern classics as well as
many contemporary pieces.

Vladimir Kagan Classic Collection
P. O. Box 6464
New York
NY 10128-0008
212-289-0031
www.kaganfurnitureclassics.com
Mid-century modern pieces by Vladimir
Kagan, including designs from the 1940s,
1950s, and 1960s as well as contemporary
pieces. Visit their website for stockists.

Knoll International
105 Wooster Street
New York
NY 10012
212-343-4000
www.knoll.com
Classic twentieth-century pieces by Mies
van der Rohe, Eero Saarinen, Harry Bertoia,
and Florence Knoll, among many others.

Lost City Arts
275 Lafayette Street
New York
NY 10012
212-941-8025
Original and re-issued design classics from
the 1930s to the 1960s.

Machine Age
354 Congress Street
Boston
MA 02210
617-482-0048
Furniture from the 1940s to the 1970s.

Mecca Modern Interior
21a South Broadway
Denver
CO 80209
888-307-2600
www.meccainterior.com
The finest Modern and Postmodern
European design classics.

Mode Moderne
159 North 3rd Street
Philadelphia
PA 19105
215-627-0299
www.modemoderne.com
Mid-century modern furnishings.

Modernica
57 Greene Street
New York
NY 10012
212-219-1303
Modern classics from Herman Miller, Ligne
Roset, and Artemide, as well as their own
range of contemporary pieces.

Modern Age
102 Wooster Street
New York
NY 10012
212-966-0669
A selection of modern classics.

Modern House
7924 Lorain Avenue
Cleveland
OH 44102
216-651-3040
Vintage modern furnishings.

Modern Times
1538 North Milwaukee
Chicago
IL 60622
773-772-8871
Twentieth-century home furnishings.

Modern Way
1426 North Palm Canyon Drive
Palm Springs
California 92262
760-320-5455
Furniture from the 1940s to the 1970s.

The Morson Collection
100 East Walton Street
Chicago
IL 60611
312-587-7400
and at
31 St James Avenue
Boston
MA 02116
617-482-2335
Modern classic furniture and lighting. Call
800 204 2514 if located outside of Illinois
and Massachusetts.

Quasi Modo
789 Queen Street West
M6J IGI
Toronto, Ontario
Canada
416-703-8300
Re-editions of modern classics by designers
such as Charles and Ray Eames and Isamu
Noguchi.

ReGeneration
38 Renwick Street
New York
NY 10013
212-741-2102
email:regen@interport.net
www.regenerationfurniture.com
Three floors of furniture from the 1950s
and 1960s.

RetroModern
www.retromodern.com
An internet superstore of twentieth-century
design, offering both new and vintage
pieces. Also tableware, design books, and
a gift registry.

Senzatempo
815 Washington Avenue
Miami Beach
FL 33139
800-408-8419
Designs by Charles and Ray Eames, George
Nelson, Alvar Aalto, and more.

Shaboom's
5533 West Glendale Avenue
Glendale
AZ 85301
602-842-8687
Twentieth-century classic furniture and
decorative arts.

Swank
45 East 7th Street
New York
NY 10003
212-673-8597
www.swank-nyc.com
New and vintage twentieth-century classics.

Weinberg
84 Wooster Street
New York
NY 10012
212-219-3022
Fine original pieces of twentieth-century
design.

**Architects and designers whose work
has been featured in this book:**

Azman Owens Architects
8 St Albans Place
London N1 0NX
011 44 20 7354 2955
fax: 011 44 20 7354 2955
email: azmanowens.com
Pages 4 & 5, 40 & 41 al,46,
50 al, 55 al & br, 78 bl, 117

Michael Benevento
Orange Group
515 Broadway
New York
NY 10012
212-965-8617
Pages 34, 35 al, 37 r, 41 ac & ar, 114–115 b,
126–127 & 127 b

Bilhuber Inc.
330 East 59th Street
6th Floor
New York
NY 10022
212-308-4888
Page 19 al

Brookes Stacey Randall
New Hibernia House
Winchester Walk
London SE1 9AG
011 44 20 7403 0707
Page 36 br

Ian Chee VX Designs
011 44 20 7370 5496
Pages 21 ar, 27 r, 68–69 a, 71

Justin de Syllas
Avanti Architects Ltd.
1 Torriano Mews
London NW5 2RZ
011 44 20 7284 1616
Pages 21 cr, 24–25 a

Nanna Ditzel MDD FCSD
Industrial designer specializing
in furniture, textiles, jewellery
and exhibitions.
Nanna Ditzel Design
Klareboderne 4
DK-1115 Copenhagen K
www.nanna-ditzel-design.dk
Pages 56 b, 57 al & bl, 108 l,
114–115 a, 132 br

Full House
38 Renwick St
New York
NY 10013
646-486-4151
Pages 36 ar, 37 l, 47 ar, 56 ar, 104–105,
116 b, 119 b

Steven Learner Studio
138 West 25th Street
12th Floor
New York
NY 10001
212-741-8583
Pages 134–135

Marino + Giolito
161 West 16th Street
New York
NY 10011
212-260-8142
Page 121 r

The Moderns
900 Broadway
Suite 903
New York
NY 10003
212-387-8852
fax: 212-387-8824
email: moderns@aol.com
Pages 1 & 2, 35 bl & br, 62–63, 82–83,
114 l

Johnson Naylor
011 44 20 7490 8885
email: brian.johnson@johnsonnaylor.co.uk
Pages 13 al, 21 br, 74 al

Judy Ross
Judy Ross Textiles/Carpets
1 Union Square South
New York
NY 10003
212-842-2607
Pages 1, 62–63. 82–83

John L. Stewart
SIT, L.L.C.
113–115 Bank Street
New York
NY 10014-2176
212-620-0777
fax: 212-620-0770
email: JLSCollection@aol.com
Pages 38 l, 43 r, 56 al & cl, 57 r,
66 l, 70 l, 102 & 102–103, 119 a, 136 al

Picture credits

All photographs are by Andrew Wood unless otherwise stated

1 & 2 Chelsea Loft apartment in New York, designed by The Moderns;   **3** Century, 020 7487 5100;   **4 & 5** Guido Palau's house in North London, designed by Azman Owens Architects;   **6** Century, 020 7487 5100;   **7** John Cheim's apartment in New York;   **8** Heidi Kingstone's apartment in London;   **10–11** Neil Bingham's house in Blackheath, London, chair courtesy of Designer's Guild;   **12–13** Philippe Garner;   **13 al** The penthouse at Millennium Harbour, London, designed by CZWG Architects and Johnson Naylor, photographed courtesy of Alan Selby & Partners;   **14 l** Mary Evans Picture Library;   **14 r** The Advertising Archives;   **15 al** Philippe Garner;   **15 ar** Elizabeth Whiting & Associates;   **15 bl** The Art Archive;   **15 br** Century, 020 7487 5100;   **15 c** Carpet by Da Silva Bruhns, c. 1930, private collection/The Bridgeman Art Library;   **16** Century, 020 7487 5100;   **16 b** The Advertising Archives;   **16–17** Ezra Stoller/Esto/Arcaid;   **18** Ezra Stoller/Esto/Arcaid;   **19 al** photography by Ray Main/a house in Pennsylvania designed by Jeffrey Bilhuber;   **19 ac** photography by Chris Everard;   **19 ar** courtesy of Knoll International;   **19 bl** Festival of Britain Style Fabric, early 1950s, private collection/The Bridgeman Art Library;   **19 bc & br** courtesy of Herman Miller Inc;   **20 l** courtesy of Herman Miller Inc;   **20 r** The Advertising Archives;   **21 al & cl** photography by Tam Nhu Tran;   **21 bl** 'Sea Things' textile by Ray Eames, 1945 (hand–printed silk screen on card), private collection/Bonhams/ The Bridgeman Art Library;   **21 ar** Ian Chee's apartment in London;   **21 cr** Annette Main and Justin De Syllas' house in London, chair courtesy of Fritz Hansen;   **21 br** Brian Johnson's apartment in London, designed by Johnson Naylor, chair courtesy of Race Furniture;   **22 al & ar** courtesy of Herman Miller Inc;   **22 bl** The Advertising Archives;   **22–23 & 23 a** Elizabeth Whiting & Associates;   **23 b** The Advertising Archives;   **24 bl** Three vases by G.P. Baxter for Whitefriars Glass, 1966, Glass Manufacturers Federation/The Bridgeman Art Library;   **24 bl** Christies Images Ltd;   **24–25 a** Annette Main and Justin De Syllas' house in London;   **24–25 b** Elizabeth Whiting & Associates;   **26 al, ar, bl & 26–27** Elizabeth Whiting & Associates;   **27 al** photography by Chris Everard;   **27 r** Ian Chee's apartment in London, chair courtesy of Vitra;   **28 b** Elizabeth Whiting & Associates;   **29 al, ar, bl & br** Elizabeth Whiting & Associates;   **30** Elizabeth Whiting & Associates;   **31 bl** photography by Chris Everard/light courtesy of Skandium;   **31 ar & br** Elizabeth Whiting & Associates;   **34 & 35 al** Michael Benevento – Orange Group;   **35 ar** John Cheim's apartment in New York;   **35 bl & br** Chelsea Loft apartment in New York, designed by The Moderns;   **36 ar** Apartment of Michel Hurst/Robert Swope, owners of Full House NYC; **36 bl** Kurt Bredenbeck's apartment at the Barbican, London;   **36 br** Freddie Daniells' loft in London, designed by Brookes Stacey Randall;   **37 l** Apartment of Michel Hurst/Robert Swope, owners of Full House NYC;   **37 r** Michael Benevento – Orange Group;   **38 l** An apartment in The San Remo on the Upper West Side of Manhattan, designed by John L. Stewart and Michael D'Arcy of SIT;   **38 r & 39** Century, 020 7487 5100;   **40 & 41 al** Guido Palau's house in North London, designed by Azman Owens Architects;   **41 ac & ar** Michael Benevento – Orange Group;   **41 b** Jo Shane, John Cooper, and family, apartment in New York;   **42 ar, bl & 42–43** John Cheim's apartment in New York;   **43 r** An apartment in The San Remo on the Upper West Side of Manhattan, designed by John L. Stewart and Michael D'Arcy of SIT;   **44 al** Phillip Low, New York;   **44 b, 44–45, 45 a & c** Century, 020 7487 5100;   **46** Guido Palau's house in North London, designed by Azman Owens Architects;   **47 al** John Cheim's apartment in New York;   **47 ar** Apartment of Michel Hurst/Robert Swope, owners of Full House NYC;   **47 br** Kurt Bredenbeck's apartment at the Barbican, London;   **48 a** Heidi Kingstone's apartment in London;   **48 b** Jane Collins of Sixty 6 in Marylebone High Street, home in central London;   **50 al** Guido Palau's house in North London, designed by Azman Owens Architects;   **50 ar & 51 r** Jane Collins of Sixty 6 in Marylebone High Street, home in central London;   **52 bl** Jo Shane, John Cooper, and family, apartment in New York;   **53 r** John Cheim's apartment in New York;   **54 a & b** Jane Collins of Sixty 6 in Marylebone High Street, home in central London;   **54–55** Phillip Low, New York; **55 al & br** Guido Palau's house in North London, designed by Azman Owens Architects;   **55 ar & bl** Phillip Low, New York;   **56 al & cl** An apartment in The San Remo on the Upper West Side of Manhattan, designed by John L. Stewart and Michael D'Arcy of SIT;   **56 ar** Apartment of Michel Hurst/Robert

Swope, owners of Full House NYC; **56 b, 57 al & bl** Nanna Ditzel's home in Copenhagen; **57 r** An apartment in The San Remo on the Upper West Side of Manhattan, designed by John L. Stewart and Michael D'Arcy of SIT; **58–59 & 59** Jane Collins of Sixty 6 in Marylebone High Street, home in central London; **62–63** Chelsea Loft apartment in New York, designed by The Moderns; **65 r** Jane Collins of Sixty 6 in Marylebone High Street, home in central London; **66 l** An apartment in The San Remo on the Upper West Side of Manhattan, designed by John L. Stewart and Michael D'Arcy of SIT; **66 r** Jane Collins of Sixty 6 in Marylebone High Street, home in central London; **67** Century, 020 7487 5100; **68 l** Neil Bingham's house in Blackheath, London; **68–69 a** photography by Tam Nhu Tran/Ian Chee's apartment in London; **68–69 b & 69 a** photography by Polly Wreford; **69 b** Neil Bingham's house in Blackheath, London; **70 l** An apartment in The San Remo on the Upper West Side of Manhattan, designed by John L. Stewart and Michael D'Arcy of SIT; **70 r** Jane Collins of Sixty 6 in Marylebone High Street, home in central London; **71** photography by Tam Nhu Tran/Ian Chee's apartment in London; **72 l, ar, br & 73** Century, 020 7487 5100; **74 al** photography by Tam Nhu Tran/Brian Johnson's apartment in London, designed by Johnson Naylor; **74 ar & br** photography by Tam Nhu Tran; **74 bl** photography by Tom Leighton; **75 al, c & b** photography by Tam Nhu Tran; **75 ar** John Cheim's apartment in New York; **76** Norma Holland's house in London; **77 al** Jo Shane, John Cooper, and family, apartment in New York; **77 r** Kurt Bredenbeck's apartment at the Barbican, London; **78 al** photography by Polly Wreford; **78 alc** Neil Bingham's House in Blackheath, London; **78 arc, mc, brc & br** photography by Tam Nhu Tran; **78 ar** Phillip Low, New York; **78 bl** Guido Palau's

house in North London, designed by Azman Owens Architects; **79 l** Century, 020 7487 5100; **79 ar** photography by Polly Wreford/an apartment in New York designed by Belmont Freeman Architects; **79 b** photography by Polly Wreford; **80 l & r** Jo Shane, John Cooper, and family, apartment in New York; **80–81 & 81** Neil Bingham's house in Blackheath, London; **82–83** Chelsea Loft apartment in New York, designed by The Moderns; **86 & 87** Jane Collins of Sixty 6 in Marylebone High Street, home in central London; **88–89** Norma Holland's house in London; **90–91 & 91** John Cheim's apartment in New York; **94 l** Century, 020 7487 5100; **96–97 & 97** Century, 020 7487 5100; **98–99** Heidi Kingstone's apartment in London; **100–101** Jo Shane, John Cooper, and family, apartment in New York; **102 & 102–103** An apartment in The San Remo on the Upper West Side of Manhattan, designed by John L. Stewart and Michael D'Arcy of SIT; **104–105** Apartment of Michel Hurst/Robert Swope, owners of Full House NYC; **106** Kurt Bredenbeck's apartment at the Barbican, London; **107 bl & r** Heidi Kingstone's apartment in London; **108 l** Nanna Ditzel's home in Copenhagen; **108–109** Neil Bingham's house in Blackheath, London; **109 r** Jane Collins of Sixty 6 in Marylebone High Street, home in central London; **110–111** Norma Holland's house in London; **112 & 112–113** Phillip Low, New York; **114 l** Chelsea Loft apartment in New York, designed by The Moderns; **114–115 a** Nanna Ditzel's home in Copenhagen; **114–115 b** Michael Benevento – Orange Group; **116 al** Century, 020 7487 5100; **116 b** Apartment of Michel Hurst/Robert Swope, owners of Full House NYC; **117** Guido Palau's house in North London, designed by Azman Owens Architects; **119 a** An apartment in The San Remo

on the Upper West Side of Manhattan, designed by John L. Stewart and Michael D'Arcy of SIT; **119 b** Apartment of Michel Hurst/Robert Swope, owners of Full House NYC; **120 & 120–121** Century, 020 7487 5100; **121 r** Chelsea Studio New York City, designed by Marino and Giolito; **122 main** Century, 020 7487 5100; **123** Kurt Bredenbeck's apartment at the Barbican, London; **124** Phillip Low, New York; **125 al** Jo Shane, John Cooper, and family, apartment in New York; **125 bl** Heidi Kingstone's apartment in London; **125 br** photography by Polly Wreford/an apartment in New York designed by Belmont Freeman Architects; **126–127 & 127 b** Michael Benevento – Orange Group; **127 a** Century, 020 7487 5100; **128 br** John Cheim's apartment in New York; **128–129** Jo Shane, John Cooper, and family, apartment in New York; **129 bl & r** Century, 020 7487 5100; **130–131** John Cheim's apartment in New York; **132 al** Jo Shane, John Cooper, and family, apartment in New York; **132 ar** Heidi Kingstone's apartment in London; **132 br** Nanna Ditzel's home in Copenhagen; **133** Kurt Bredenbeck's apartment at the Barbican, London; **134–135** The loft of Peggy & Steven Learner, designed by Steven Learner Studio; **136 al** An apartment in The San Remo on the Upper West Side of Manhattan, designed by John L. Stewart and Michael D'Arcy of SIT; **136 bl** Heidi Kingstone's apartment in London; **136 r** Century, 020 7487 5100; **137** John Cheim's apartment in New York; **144 l** John Cheim's apartment in New York; **144 c & r** Jane Collins of Sixty 6 in Marylebone High Street, home in central London.

Index

acknowledgments

Neil Bingham would like to warmly thank Luis Peral Aranda for his invaluable contribution towards the concept of this book; Eleanor Gawne for her perceptive comments on the text; and Paul Agnew and Peter Fuller for their support. Also to my sister and brother-in-law, Lynne and Miro, who made the meals while I was writing. My colleagues at the Drawings Collection and Library of the Royal Institute of British Architects were always quick to fill gaps in knowledge during my research. Over the years, many dealers and collectors have become dear friends, and I thank them for their enthusiastic appreciation. The perceptive eye and good humor of my coauthor, Andrew Weaving, greatly enriched the writing of my captions.

Andrew Weaving would like to thank everyone who helped with the locations, especially those who let us into their homes. Special thanks to Michael Benevento and Stuart Basseches for their introductions. And, of course, thanks to Ian, Spot, and Zachary for their support.